D1101030

FOUR LETTER WORDS

Conversations on Faith's Beauty and Logic

by
Bill Giovannetti

Foreword by
Ken Cleaver, Ph.D.
Chair, Department of Theology, School of Religion
Liberty University

© Copyright Bill Giovannetti 2012. All Rights Reserved

Printed and bound in the United States of America. No part of this book may be reproduced or transmitted in any form or by any means, digital, electronic or mechanical, including photocopying, recording, or by an information storage and retrieval system—except by a reviewer who may quote brief passages in a review to be printed in a magazine, newspaper, or on the Web—without permission in writing from the publisher. For information, please contact Endurant Press, PO Box 670, Shasta, CA 96087 or info@fourletterwords.org.

Although the author and publisher have made every effort to ensure the accuracy and completeness of information contained in this book, the same assumes no responsibility for errors, inaccuracies, omissions, or any inconsistency herein. Any slights of people, places, or organizations are unintentional. All persons and situations mentioned in this book are fictionalized. Any resemblance to any person, living or dead, is strictly coincidental. Nothing herein shall be construed as a substitute for personal, pastoral, or professional counseling or therapy.

First Printing 2011.
Printed in the U.S.A.

Printed on SFI certified paper from sustainable and responsible sources.

ISBN: 978-0-9836812-6-7
(e-book: 978-0-9836812-0-5)

Library of Congress Control Number: 2011931902

Cover design: Walker Creative 2011. Interior Design: Endurant Press. Cover title font: Blackout, copyright Tyler Finck 2008. Used by permission. www.sursly.com. Title font: The Battle Continues, copyright CHEC 2003. Used by permission.

All scripture quotations, unless otherwise indicated, are taken from the *New King James Version* (R). Copyright © 1982 by Thomas Nelson, Inc. Used by permission. All rights reserved.

Scripture quotations marked (NLT) are taken from the *Holy Bible, New Living Translation,* copyright © 1996, 2004, 2007 by Tyndale House Foundation. Used by permission of Tyndale House Publishers, Inc., Carol Stream, Illinois 60188. All rights reserved.

ATTENTION CORPORATIONS, UNIVERSITIES, COLLEGES, CHURCHES and MINISTRY GROUPS: Quantity discounts are availble on bulk purchases of this book for educational, gift purposes, group studies, or premiums. Special books or book excerpts can also be created to fit specific needs. Please contact info@FourLetterWords.org for information.

What Readers Are Saying...

"I don't know if you were hoping for a rave review or not but... you've got it. This was great. Seriously. I was tempted to pass it on to my pastor because I think it is something he really needs to read. Our neighborhood is all young, postmodern-ish people, VERY reluctant to go to a church with "evangelical" over the door. I read it all through a couple times, my husband read it through and we agreed that it's a really important and well-written book. Your voice is great. You are making whole semesters worth of information very accessible. Huge high-five directed your way." --Amy and Wayne, legal assistant and coffee barista, Chicago

-----&*%$@%f**-----

"Well, I love it. You hit the nail on the head with the conversational aspect. It is easy to read, witty, funny, and clever without skimping on meat. Most importantly, as a 20 something majoring in philosophy and in love with Biblical theology, I would recommend this book at length to anyone and everyone I know. Like I said before, it is weighty enough to captivate people versed in philosophical nomenclature without disappointment, and yet practical enough for your average blue-collar guy or gal to grasp and utilize. Our culture is indeed under attack, and we need to provide the tools of battle needed to wage war. This is one of those tools, and I thank God that He has given you the ability to do something like this."

"You accurately and passionately take very deep, very profound theological and philosophical concepts and give them a familiarity that would allow me to be on a first name basis with them. -- Drew Mitchell, philosophy major and seminarian

-----&*%$@%f**-----

"With this book Bill Giovannetti has met the Biblical mandate to 'speak the truth in love.' *Four Letter Words* serves up the truth (even when it hurts), but delivers it with such grace that the compassionate heart of God beats from cover to cover. Get this book for every student your life." -- Dave Meurer, author of *Mistake It Like a Man* and *The Hair-Raising Joys of Raising Boys*

"I have several four letter words to describe Bill Giovannetti's fresh work, *Four-Letter Words*. As a teacher of philosophy at a secular college and apologetics at a seminary, I would first speak of *need*. This is a much needed volume because of two qualities I greatly appreciate. It is *deep* in the unique sense that it backfills that huge gap that our philosophically and theologically illiterate world reveals. Because so many today lack the intellectual foundation for meaningful discussion, Bill not only frames the debate, but provides a much needed foundation. And I found the material *real* – transparent, honest, and uncompromised." -- Dr. Bob Wenz, Ravi Zacharias International Ministries, Adjunct Faculty

DEDICATIONS

Every time I think of you, I give thanks to my God.
(Philippians 1:3, NLT).

For Josie and J.D. May you always know the love of Jesus, enjoy life with God, and live for him. May your future spouses, your children and children's children, glorify God and enjoy him forever. Your Dad loves you forever.

For the people of Neighborhood Church, Grace Pointe Church, Grace Gospel Church, and Windy City Community Church. I have no greater joy than to hear that my friends walk in truth. (3 John 4)

For the AWANA Youth Association, Art Roreheim, and Lance B. Latham, thank you for filling my childhood mind with the living and abiding Word of God.

For apologists Ravi Zacharias, John Ankerberg, Norman Geisler, Josh McDowell, C.S. Lewis, and Erwin Lutzer, thank you for leading me to the full assurance of faith.

For Amy & Wayne Giacalone, Jonathan Heaps, Chris Griffin, Jordan Aman, and Drew Mitchell, thank you for your encouragement and valuable suggestions.

For A.W. Tozer Theological Seminary, Simspon University, and the Christian and Missionary Alliance, thank you for giving me a family of faith.

For my mom, Dorothy—thank you for a lifetime of sacrificial love. And my late father, Roy B. Giovannetti—thank you for getting baptized at 83 and making sure we knew you knew God. See you soon.

For Margi, the love of my life, thank you for choosing me. I choose you back over and over again.

FOREWORD

by
Ken Cleaver, Ph.D.

"And if you are asked about your Christian hope, always be ready to explain it." (1 Peter 3:15b, NLT)

During my childhood years, most everyone around me was a Christian. I was raised in a Christian home, attended a Christian church and its school, had mostly Christian friends, and spent most of my nights, weekends, and summers with Christians too. My Christian teachers did a great job at teaching me the content of the Bible, and over the years I memorized many of its verses.

Although my faith in God and His Word was real, I was missing something crucial. I seemed to "crash and burn" every time I tried to explain my faith to a non-Christian friend or answer their tough questions about God and life. I had been taught nice, neat, tidy Sunday school answers to the easier questions, but the tougher questions on touchy subjects asked outside of the church walls posed a formidable challenge for me.

Outside of the church walls the authority of the Bible was not assumed, and God's choices—especially about suffering and evil—were questioned. For that matter, even the idea of absolute truth or the existence of God was doubted. How was I supposed to have a serious conversation with someone about God or life, if we could not even agree on a common source of authority? Sure, I could quote Bible verses to them, but they would respond, "so what?" or "how do I know that's true?"

In the face of these tough challenges, it seemed like there were only two choices: (a) run away or (b) figure out a better way to answer the world's tough questions. Those who run away cannot help the people who ask the tough questions. The Bible encourages us: "And if you are asked about your Christian hope, always be ready to explain it. But you must do this in a gentle and respectful way (1 Peter 3:15, 16, NLT)."

The questions will be asked whether we are prepared or not.

- Are you ready to explain the truth to people who deny it can be known, your faith to those who see faith as a weakness, and your hope to those who have lost hope?
- When someone asks you how a good and powerful God could allow suffering and evil to continue in the world, will you know how to respond?
- Are you prepared to show how God's Word and His love address the deepest and broadest concerns of our lives?
- Beyond having good answers to tough questions on touchy subjects, are you yourself convinced that your answers are true?

In *Four Letter Words* Bill Giovannetti gets right to the heart of these matters and equips Christians with well-thought-out ideas about how to turn challenges to our faith into opportunities to share God's love and truth to a generation in need of Him. You will come away from this book not only better prepared to answer questions but also greatly encouraged in the truth and power of your faith. We do not need to be ashamed of the good news about Jesus! As a matter of fact, that good news is the power of God at work to save everyone who believes from their sin (Romans 1:16).

The truth does not restrict us; it frees us to think and live the way we were designed to in the first place.

I appreciate the way that Giovannetti deals directly with tough issues on touchy subjects. He answers difficult questions with straightforward language and ideas. You will not need a seminary degree to read this book, but you may feel like you got one when you are done reading it. I highly recommend this book to all who want to be ready to answer questions about the Christian faith.

Ken Cleaver, Ph.D.
Chairman, Department of Theology
Liberty University

CONTENTS

CHAPTER I

FOUR LETTER WORDS

When angry, count four. When very angry, swear.
MARK TWAIN

I F MANY OF OUR FRIENDS HAD THEIR WAY, Christ's followers would be walking around with a bar of soap stuck in their mouths. When a graduation prayer becomes a federal case, and major department stores censor a festive "Merry Christmas," you might suspect new standards for verbal vulgarity.

The core beliefs of the Christian faith have become today's four letter words. Annoyed by the Christ-follower's "narrow-mindedness," our politically correct culture enforces a highly selective tolerance: fist-bumping any philosophical fad and moral deviation as long as it's not in harmony with Grandma's leather Bible.

Endorsing her old-fashioned religion might get you sent to your room without any supper.

Take, for example, my recent unwitting obscenity against a friend. I didn't mean to be a jerk, and I certainly didn't plan to get on her nerves. But my friend rolled her eyes and our conversation dropped off a cliff. My only crime was to say that I belonged to God because I had Jesus. "Jesus" got me the dreaded eye-roll. My friend didn't object to my belief as much as to my confidence.

To her, it smelled like arrogance.

Our conversation turned testy. We changed subjects. I still tiptoe around God when she's around.

When did Jesus-talk become dirty? If I had cursed my friend like Blackbeard's parrot, she would have been less offended. Talking about faith in general might be cool, but in many quarters, to express that faith in terms of traditional Christian values—concerning sex, truth, hell, and salvation—is to smash a cultural taboo.

Talk like that too much and you'll get your mouth washed out with soap.

This book is about struggle. Not between good and evil or right and wrong. Not the clash of religions. Not some kind of cosmic warfare between God and Satan. It is about the very personal struggle each of us faces as we grapple with faith, reality, sexuality, life, and death.

I'm not trying to win any wars with this book. I'm just offering my confession of how I wrestled with my inner contradictions and arrived at a certain level of peace.

In 2008, Christians cheered when *American Idol* contestants performed the worship song, "Shout to the Lord." Many viewers didn't notice that they sang the song two days in a row and not the same way each time.

The first performance dropped the name of Jesus, singing, "My *Shepherd*, my Savior, Lord there is none like you..." Perhaps due to an avalanche of complaints, or perhaps due to a change of conscience—the producers haven't explained why—the second performance reverted to the original lyrics: "My *Jesus*, My Savior, Lord there is none like you..."

powered by BWSCAN.com
"Shout to the Lord"

"Shout to the Lord" was one of the great worship songs of its generation. I was happy to see it performed. But the way Christians over-responded was a bit embarrassing. Churches celebrated, bloggers gushed, and Christians lit up the FOX switchboards in appreciation. You would have thought we had just won the Superbowl—all because Jesus got a mention on the secular media.

I'm all for that, but... aren't we behaving like the team's scrawny benchwarmer—giddy to take the field for the last minute, even though game is just about over? Do we now imagine that the rest of the team respects us because we got sixty seconds of playing time?

They don't.

It's The End of the World As We Know It

Some experts suggest we're living at the tail end of Christendom—the period when Christianity captained the cultural team. We live in a "post-Christian era," they say. The Bible-centered worldview that shaped Western civilization since the Magna Carta (1215) has fizzled in the face of an ultra-tolerant diversity that remains perpetually ticked off at Christians.

"Shout to the Lord" on *American Idol* has as much meaning as "Amazing Grace" at a drug-dealer's funeral.

Yes, we're glad when Jesus is honored. But we recognize that authentic Christ-followers are a shrinking minority among neighbors who might grab onto Jesus in an emergency, but otherwise don't want him "crammed down their throats."

There has never been a culture more desperate for answers to life's big questions, and never a culture more convinced no answers exist.

This makes following Jesus really tough, especially for younger Christians. It's painful to watch our culture, and many of our friends, first value, then ignore, and finally turn against a Christian worldview.

Thou shalt tolerate every opinion... except the Christian's. Today's postmodern "prime directive" leaves many followers of Jesus tongue-tied. In the global village, isn't it unreasonable—and even danger-ous—to suggest that the Bible has a monopoly on truth?

The church needs a new breed of Christ-follower. We need Christ-followers who are alert to today's touchy ideas—the truths that fire up more heat than light. We need Christ-followers who can make a clear case for the Bible's worldview; who are ready to help our friends think through their beliefs; who can recognize inconsisten-cies and challenge them; and who can do all of this with humility, confidence, humor, and love.

What if the only reason Christ's message offends is that it wounds our misplaced pride in ourselves?

And what if it's exactly that wound that launches our quest for healing?

No religion has ever offered as plausible or beautiful a worldview as historic, biblical Christianity. Let's say so.

Four Letter Words shows how. I wrote it to teach Christ's followers to cuss boldly—to speak faith's four letter words—without backing down, yet without coming across as a religious inquisitor either. I want to help you talk about your faith. And I want to strengthen that faith and convince you deep inside that Jesus is a treasure worth sharing.

When Jesus spotlighted himself as ultimate truth, the Religious Establishment painted a bullseye on his back.

When he highlighted their hypocrisy, they picked up stones to kill him.

When he stood silent, showing up the insanity of their rage, they nailed him to the cross.

When he prayed, "Father forgive them," they played games with his shredded robe, making it a hideous souvenir.

There was nothing Jesus could say or do—short of redefining himself to suit their preconceptions—to make everybody like him. So he stood strong, kept the faith, spoke the truth, loved the world, and let God handle the outcomes.

Such a life was interpreted by most as a long string of four letter words. It always will be.

But one man, standing at the foot of the cross, heard it differently. He was a Roman centurion, part of the squad that crucified Jesus.

He said, "Truly, this man was the Son of God" (Mark 13:39).

He was only the first of countless seekers who saw the cross, not as a lunatic's curse, but as heaven's blessing.

May your life story speak forth that blessing for countless seekers more.

------ # & ! $ # + % ----

CLICK IT: www.FourLetterWords.org.

SCAN IT:

powered by BWSCAN.com

What is truth? said jesting Pilate, but would not stay
for an answer.

S͏IR F͏RANCIS B͏ACON, A.D. 1625

Touchy Ideas

1. Some ideas are true and some ideas are false.
2. When an idea is true for one person, it's true for everybody.
3. Truth is absolute, for all times and places.
4. A fact can't be both true and false at the same time.
5. When two ideas contradict each other, they can't both be true.
6. Biblical Christianity is true.
7. Whenever other religions contradict biblical Christianity, they're false.

Touchy Scriptures

1. Jesus said to him, "I am the way, the truth, and the life. No one comes to the Father except through Me." (John 14:6)
2. And the Word became flesh and dwelt among us, and we beheld His glory, the glory as of the only begotten of the Father, full of grace and truth. (John 1:14)
3. And this is eternal life, that they may know You, the only true God, and Jesus Christ whom You have sent. (John 17:3).

------ # & ! $ # + % ----

What is Truth?

"Let God be true, but every man a liar."
Romans 3:4

SOME THINGS ARE TRUE. Some things are false. You might get an argument about that.

Our church's worship team was first confused and then angry when they discovered a major theft. Burglars had broken into our northern California church and ripped off a truckload of instruments and electronic equipment worth tens of thousands of dollars.

When they arrived for their final run-through, our worship team found the stage stripped bare. They borrowed some instruments and led us in a great time of worship, but we still felt violated. During our worship times, we prayed for the bad guys—that God would melt their hard hearts and drive them to turn themselves in.

Among other things, the thieves stole an entire drum kit. Later that week, one of our drummers, Jeff, found a used drum kit on craigslist, a classified ad website. Jeff drove to the seller's house, negotiated a fair price and struck a deal. As he was loading the drums into his car, Jeff mentioned that he would play them at church.

The seller said, "Oh! This is for a church? Great! I'll knock off a hundred bucks."

Jeff thought, How cool! This guy must be a Christian.

His warm fuzzies popped like a balloon when the seller added: "...because Jesus is one of my gurus, too."

Yes, it was very nice of the seller to reduce his price for us. We're grateful for that; I celebrate every time a spiritual door opens in anybody's life. At the same time, I cringe when Jesus gets clumped together with the world's gurus, as if he were just one option among equals. The drum-seller displayed a common attitude toward truth in today's culture. It's the attitude that suggests that mutually contradictory ideas can both be true at the same time, in the same way.

This doesn't make sense, and it doesn't work in real life. Let me explain why by laying out two commonsense realities called Consistency and Non-Contradiction.

Consistency

Most philosophers credit Socrates for first stating that a belief can't be both true and not true at the same time. When we speak, we expect intelligent listeners to hear our words the way we mean them.[1]

If I say Chicago, deep-dish pizza is the best pizza in the world, then it is nonsense for me to say that it is not  the best pizza in the world. If a thought could be both true and false at the same time, then we live in an absurd universe. Even worse, everything you tell me would be suspect because I would have no way of figuring out if it were true or false.

Experts in logic call this *consistency*. Unless we want to skip straight to a throbbing headache, we have to agree that a truth, belief, idea, proposition, or assertion is always consistent with itself. If this were not the case, then I could tell you I love you but actually hate you and not be lying.

How crazy that would be! Imagine a first date...

YOU: You look really nice tonight. Great shoes, too.

YOUR DATE: You hate me, don't you?

YOU: What do you mean, "I hate you?" I just said you

look nice. Really nice. I'm happy to be going out with you.

YOUR DATE: Ah-ha! You're still thinking about your last relationship with Chris. I knew this was a mistake.

YOU: B-b-but... I always thought you were great, and- and, uhhh... I was happy about our date.

YOUR DATE: My mother warned me about people like you...

YOU: You're crazy.

YOUR DATE: *(suddenly happy)* Oh! Thanks. I think you're great too. So, where should we go for dinner?

The law of consistency keeps us out of the loony bin.

This is important for followers of Jesus. Truth makes sense. Every truth is consistent with itself because all truth flows from God; he is the fixed point in a universe in motion.

Even more, every truth should be consistent with every other truth. This is where things get hairy with our skeptical friends.

Non-contradiction

Two contradictory beliefs can't both be right. Normal people know this. This is called the *principle of non-contradiction* (PNC). It reminds us of what we all know intuitively: that contradictory statements can't both be true. If I tell you that *Starbucks* is two blocks up and to the left, and a street musician says it's two blocks up and to the right, and we're talking about the same coffee shop from the same starting point, at least one of us is wrong.

An ancient Persian scholar, Avicenna the Physician,[2] defended the PNC in a politically incorrect and morally horrific—though really persuasive—way, when he wrote,

Anyone who denies the law of non-contradiction should be beaten and burned until he admits that to be beaten is not the same as not to be beaten, and to be burned is not the same as not to be burned.[3]

Ouch.

We couldn't make it through a single day without trusting the principle of non-contradiction. Everybody knows this stuff. Everybody lives by it. No sane people question it. Until we come to religion.

Then, many skeptics shed logic like my dog sheds fur.

A prime example:

- *Atheists* say there is no God.
- *The ancient Romans* worshiped a pantheon of gods (a whole bunch of them).
- *Muslims* teach a single, all-powerful god, called Allah.
- *Christians* maintain that there is one and only one God, who exists as a Trinity and has a divine-human Son named Jesus.

There's no way they can all be true.

Here's another example: Although some who called themselves Christian justified abuses like slavery and the subjugation of women from the Bible, they finally gave in to the relentless biblical arguments that God created all humans equal. While I grieve over those abuses, I also recognize that it was mainly Christians who abolished slavery in the western world[4] and who first recognized the essential equality of men and women.[5] St. Paul gave voice to Jesus' message when he wrote, "There is neither Jew nor Greek, there is neither slave nor free, there is neither male nor female; for you are all one in Christ Jesus" (Galatians 3:28).

Meanwhile some religions still require women to walk behind their men and to cloak themselves from head to toe, while caste-oriented religions still justify child slavery.

My point is not to condemn followers of these religions. I feel compassion for these people. My point is to show that these religions contradict each other on important issues: God, human dignity, ethics, how we treat each other, how we interface with God, how we steward our planet, and our ultimate destiny.

They can't all be right. The logic that guides our everyday lives says so.

It's at this point that many of our friends hop off the train of rationality by suggesting that religions all say the same things. Really? How can religions say the same things when they actually say opposite things? Can the law of contradiction ever take a vacation?

And isn't it at least a little inconsistent for professors or friends to argue that all religions say the same thing, and then to disagree with yours?

Jesus drew a dividing line between truth and falsehood: "You are of your father the devil...He... does not stand in the truth, because there is no truth in him. When he speaks a lie, he speaks from his own resources, for he is a liar and the father of it" (John 8:44). I guess, to Jesus, some ideas were true and some ideas were false.

Unfortunately, the devil's lies are alive and well in our classrooms and neighborhoods today. But they're subtle. Our friends and professors aren't trying to be deceitful; they're trying to be true. But society bent the mental playing field out of shape during the middle of the game. It happened so fast we hardly noticed.

Generations of Christians clipped cluelessly along, assuming that everybody agreed with them and believed like them and respected them. They never noticed when the surrounding culture first questioned, then doubted, then discarded, and finally inverted their most cherished beliefs.

While the church slept, truth and falsehood got married. Good and evil became one. And hell became a suburb of heaven. How did this happen?

Enter postmodernism, the rebellious offspring of modernism. Let me give you a brief and painless description of how both "-isms" approach truth, and then see how they stack up against biblical Christianity.

Modernism

God's way seems foolish to the Jews because they want a sign from heaven to prove it is true. And it is foolish to the Greeks because they believe only what agrees with their own wisdom.
(1 Corinthians 1:22, NLT)

I grew up running around a small church in Chicago. I was a Christian and assumed that anybody who wasn't a Christian just hadn't thought about it enough. The biblical message made sense to me.

Until high school.

Then, I faced my first crisis of faith.

I began to doubt Christianity because I couldn't reconcile the Bible with evolution. The Bible told me God created the universe and fashioned Adam and Eve. Science told me that a Big Bang created the universe, and then all life evolved from it.

I couldn't put the two together. Yes, many excellent Christians believe God himself guided the process of evolution. This book isn't about evolution, so I won't get into that. But, for my struggle at that time, *theistic evolution* (God-guided evolution) didn't work.

I came very close to abandoning Christianity because of a scientific theory. Science, as I had been taught it, undermined my faith. The story ends on a spiritual high note, however, because I studied the topic and wrote a term paper that satisfied my doubts and reassured my faith.

We'll let science represent a worldview called "modernism." This worldview tells us that truth comes from scientific or mathematical exploration. If science can't observe it, measure it, or put it into a formula, then we can't claim a belief as true. So, to a committed modernist, Moses didn't part the Red Sea, Jesus didn't walk on water, and nobody rose from the dead.

To its credit, modernism has led to advances in medicine, agriculture, engineering and virtually every other field, making life easier and healthier. Christians affirm much of modernism, because it reflects the human rationality that flows from the massive intelligence of God.

However, modernism chokes on its own I.Q. It forgets that we couldn't think at all unless God thought first. So modernism thought itself smarter than God, and reasoned him out of existence. That put modernism in the awkward position of having to explain beings like us that have more intelligence than whatever made us. The solution? Define all intelligence as a freak convergence of impersonal forces. That definition had the unintended consequence of robbing humankind of its dignity, but we'll save that for later.

It also explains why my teachers presented evolution with no room for a Creator. Modernism, in the end, undermines Christianity by claiming to be the only source of truth and by denying miracles and anything supernatural. It has no use for, and no belief in, anything beyond the bounds of nature. As astronomer Carl Sagan wrote, "The Cosmos is all that is or ever was or ever will be."[6]

Postmodernism, on the other hand, snubs its nose at modernism and embraces mystery and spirituality.

Postmodernism

In those days there was no king in Israel; everyone did what was right in his own eyes. (Judges 17:6)

Postmodernism approaches truth as an all-you-can-eat buffet: pick what you like and stop when you want to. It's really not that simple, but postmodernism adopts a more fluid approach to truth than modernism ever conceived.

In a speech before the United Nations Prayer Breakfast, Christian apologist, Ravi Zacharias, described driving past the Wexner Center for the Arts at Ohio State University. He noted the unusual architecture, and was told it was "America's first postmodern building." His host explained that it was designed "with no design in mind" to reflect the fickleness of life. The building has stairways leading nowhere, columns coming down without touching the floor, a crazy girder system supporting the roof, and pillars holding up nothing.

Ravi asked his host, "So [the architect's] argument was that, if life has no purpose and design, why should the building have any design?" His host told him he was correct.

Then Ravi asked a question that could only be answered with embarrassed silence: "Did he do the same with the foundation?"[7]

Truth might seem adaptable or even optional on the surface, but once you dig, you always find it solid and unmoving. God designed our hearts to crave truth, and we're unsettled till we find it.

Postmodernism is a catch-all term for a many-headed philosophical hydra that rebels against the so-called "rigid" and "Western" logic of modernism and promotes a free-flowing approach to truth, language, and morals. Truth, language, and morals adapt to their culture, time, and place. Or, even more intense: truth, language and morals are created by their culture, time and place.

Let's look at some strengths and weaknesses of postmodernism.

Some Strengths

Humility. Nobody has a corner on postmodern truth. It's arrogant to claim you've arrived. So postmodernists, when they're at their best, project a sense of humility about their beliefs.

Mystery and Symbolism. While modernists were busy shoving the supernatural out the front door, postmodernists were busy sneaking it in through the back door. Churches with a postmodern flair don't just preach sermons, they create sensory experiences through lighting, décor, ritual, drama, music, liturgy, and dance. They don't let sterile, academic modernism spoil the spiritual party. Even old-time evangelical icon, A.W. Tozer—definitely not a postmodern preacher—pleaded for some mystery in worship.

> **"IN THE MAJORITY OF OUR MEETINGS THERE IS SCARCELY A TRACE OF REVERENT THOUGHT, NO RECOGNITION OF THE UNITY OF THE BODY, LITTLE SENSE OF THE DIVINE PRESENCE, NO MOMENT OF STILLNESS, NO SOLEMNITY, NO WONDER, NO HOLY FEAR...**[8]**"**
> **~A.W. TOZER**

Openness to Spirituality. Postmodernists, especially young adults, are flocking toward spiritual things—a great opportunity awaits if the church can figure out how to speak to that openness.

The Whole Person. Hardcore modernists focus hard on the mind. In contrast, postmodernists distribute their energy equally among emotions, relationships, lifestyle, sexuality, world-service, the mind and the spirit. Postmodern Christians—when they maintain the historic, biblical teachings of Christianity—can bring some balance back into an often right-brained, overly intellectualized church.

So the news is not all bad on the postmodern front. But it's not all good either. Here are some serious drawbacks of postmodernism's emerging philosophy.

Some Weaknesses

Skeptical about truth. When I discuss the Bible with postmodernists, the first response I expect is cynicism. They don't just doubt the Bible's truthfulness; it's tougher than that. They doubt there is any truth to begin with. Even if there is, they're skeptical we can accurately find it.

Propaganda, not truth. Postmodernists feel that we can never be truly objective because we carry a busload of biases, cultural prejudices, and the arrogance to believe that our way is the right way. Over a century ago, philosopher Friedrich Nietzsche wrote, "There are no facts, only interpretations."[9] So, when we assert that Jesus is the way to God, a postmodernist receives that—and every other claim—as just one person's interpretation.

Hesitant to take a stand, ambiguous. If we can't really be certain about truth, then we really can't take a stand on truth, can we? I think so. Maybe. I'm not sure. Ask me later. To some postmodern thinkers, truth is never black and white; it lives in ever-shifting shades of gray, and you'd have to be a Neanderthal to know anything with certainty. That's why some of their books ask more questions than supply answers. It's great to ask questions, and it's great to be humble. But when can Christ-followers take their stand on the plain reading of Scripture?

Subjective. For most of our daily lives, we assume that "truth is out there." It exists in the real world outside our minds. We don't prove this, we just assume it. So an architect or engineer calculates roof trusses by referring to data outside her own "opinion." Let's call this *objective* truth. *Subjective* truth, in contrast, suggests truth is shaped by personal tastes, opinions and feelings. Radical postmodernists are less likely to ask, "Is it true?" and more likely to ask, "Does it feel right?" But what if selling a child into prostitution feels right in some cultures, or if dumping toxins into a river feels right for some corporate CEOs? Subjectivism makes truth, therefore...

...*Relativistic.* Truth is a moving target; it depends on people, place and time. Postmodernism allows very few permanent truths—called "absolutes"—for all people, all places, and all times. That's why our postmodern friends can say that Jesus might be true for you, but not for them.

Ultra-tolerant. Because there are few, if any, absolutes, nobody's truth beats anybody else's truth. For most of Western civilization, tolerance has meant a kind-hearted, charitable, and humble attitude toward people with whom we disagree. But today's tolerance means something else; it means an unwillingness to disagree. Only a "narrow minded bigot" would criticize somebody else's truth. That's why our friends are so touchy about our Christian certainties: because just stating our opinions with confidence makes us sound arrogant.

Accepts absurdity. Think of the contradictions you have to accept to affirm that "all religions say the same thing." The fact is that all religions say mutually contradictory things; that's why there are so many of them. Christians teach a God who is a Trinity. "Blasphemy!" says Islam.[10] They can't both be right. This brings us right back to our opening touchy idea: Some things are true and some things are false. Whenever religions contradict each other, at least one of them is false. Yes, we must respect and tolerate those with whom we disagree. But we still get to disagree and say so.

OVER THREE THOUSAND YEARS AGO, God's people descended into idol worship and moral anarchy. They invented a hybrid religion by blending idol worship with the worship of the invisible God. "Everyone did what was right in his own eyes," lamented the Bible. You can almost hear that ancient critique echoing through the corridors of postmodernism.

Would Jesus be okay with this? Would he take his place alongside the religious gurus of the world as an equal? If we gathered the "gurus" and gods of history in the same room—Confucius, Mohammed, the Buddha, Mithras, Baal, Isis, the Dalai Lama, Tolle—and invited Jesus to the party, what would he do? What would he say to them? Would he greet them as partners? Would he harmonize his viewpoints with theirs?

I believe he would love them. I believe he would engage them on a personal level—he'd be interested in their lives and what kind of food they liked and how their kids were doing. I believe he'd be a friend to whoever would be a friend to him. I can almost picture him stooping to wash their feet, and telling them, "Listen, if you think this is humbling, let me tell you about a rough cross on a hill called Calvary, and the humiliation I suffered there for you."

I also believe he would challenge their thinking. Truth is reality, and reality is this: "Therefore God also has highly exalted Him and given Him the name which is above every name, that at the name of Jesus every knee should bow, of those in heaven, and of those on earth, and of those under the earth, and that every tongue should confess that Jesus Christ is Lord, to the glory of God the Father" (Philippians 2:9-11).

Jesus on Truth

It's not hard to piece together Jesus' perspective on truth from his teachings.

First, he taught that his truth was the only truth. He didn't leave even the tiniest bit of room for the idea that contradictory claims

might also be true. For example, Jesus called the Father "the only true God" and identified himself as the only true source of eternal life (John 17:3).

Jesus answered Satan's temptation by saying, "...You shall worship the LORD your God, and Him only you shall serve" (Luke 4:8). Jesus left no room for other gurus or gods. Jesus preached his message as if it were the whole truth and the only truth for all people, places, and times. His truth was exclusive truth.

That's why he could say, "I am the way, the truth, and the life. No one comes to the Father except through Me" (John 14:6). He *excluded* other ways to God.

For Jesus, at least some truths were absolute.

Even more, he offered himself as the embodiment of absolute truth. He didn't just say, "I teach the truth," he said, "I am the truth." Jesus is to truth what the sun is to our solar system. He's the center, the fixed point, the hub, and the gravitational pull. He is the reality against which all other realities are judged.

His followers agreed. When a large number of disciples betrayed Jesus, he wasn't surprised. He asked his core followers—the twelve disciples—if they were going to leave him too. Peter answered with a question: "Lord, to whom would we go? You alone have the words that give eternal life" (John 6:68, NLT). Jesus wasn't just their top choice; he was their only choice.

Second, Jesus offered his truth as the only truth that would work in the real world. He didn't offer abstract religious thinking; he offered a real foundation for a real life. Jesus was so sure, he instructed us to build our lives on his teachings. He said, "Therefore whoever hears these sayings of Mine, and does them, I will liken him to a wise man who built his house on the rock: and the rain descended, the floods came, and the winds blew and beat on that house; and it did not fall, for it was founded on the rock" (Matthew 7:24,25).

Jesus wasn't playing mind games. He wasn't an armchair philosopher. He taught truth for a real world. He promised his followers that if they followed his truth, they'd have a solid foundation for life. Plus, he warned that a life built on anyone else's truth was a life built on sand, destined for collapse (Matthew 7:27). So much for the theory that Jesus' teachings could be true for one person, but not true for another.

Ditto for Nietzsche's theory, "There are no facts, only interpretations." Neither Jesus, nor the prophets of the Old Testament, nor the apostles of the New Testament, prefaced their teachings with disclaimers, "But that's just one man's opinion" or, "Then again, what do I know?"

They believed truth, lived truth, taught truth, suffered for the truth, and expected others to receive their truth as obviously true—so much so they expected their hearers to turn away from any claim that contradicted theirs. To them, Jesus and his truth were so true, that by comparison, everyone else's truth was a lie.

And, don't forget, they died for the truth. They died rather than say, "Caesar is Lord," which, in today's English, might sound like "Jesus is one of my gurus."

Third, Jesus presented ultimate truth as a revelation from God. He said, "I don't speak on my own authority. The Father who sent me gave me his own instructions as to what I should say" (John 12:49, NLT).

Christians define truth simply: *truth is reality as God sees it.* Yes, we can learn a great deal through science, logic and experience. Yes, our culture shapes and guides our awareness of the world around us. Ultimately, though, we can only understand truth through the lens of God's revelation.

When I was a kid, my church taught me to say, "God said it. I believe it. That settles it for me." Does that mean we tossed our brains in the dumpster? No. It means that reason, logic, and science can only bring us so far. After all, you can't put angels' wings in a test tube, or mathematically prove the existence of heaven's pearly gates. Some truths—the essential truths for a spiritual life—must be revealed by God, understood by reason or experience, and received by faith. I know that can sound like a cop-out, but in the next chapter, I'd like to make the case for faith.

```
--------------------------------
     SCAN: to read every place in
       Scripture where Jesus talks
                   about truth.
--------------------------------
```
powered by BWSCAN.com

Fourth, the revelation of the True God calls for a choice. At the end of his time on earth, Jesus told his followers, "Go into all the world and preach the gospel to every creature" (Mark 16:15).

By saying "all the world" and "every creature [person]," Jesus included cultures he knew would be hostile toward him. TRANSLATION: Jesus isn't true for some but not for others; he's true for everybody. That, at least, was Jesus' opinion. He summoned the whole world to decide for or against him.

The Old Testament describes a showdown between two religions: The religion of Baal vs. the religion of Yahweh, the God of the Jews. At the story's high point, Elijah the prophet asked, "How long will you falter between two opinions? If the LORD is God, follow Him; but if Baal, follow him" (1 Kings 18:21).

For Elijah, truth about God wasn't both/and. It was either/or. You can't follow both Baal and Yahweh. Pluralism didn't work for him. And, in matters of faith, it doesn't work today. Sooner or later, a person has to choose. If the Lord, the father of Jesus Christ, is God, follow him. If not, don't. The prophet Elijah made it that simple.

So, if you're a Christ-follower, don't back down from God's truth. I'm not saying to be obnoxious about it. Nor am I suggesting you shove the truth down your friends' throats.

I'm simply saying that you have access to abiding truth for all times and places, through the written Word of God. You don't need to apologize for it. You don't need to water it down or hide it. God will prove his truth. That's his job. Your job is to learn it, understand it deeply, love it, communicate it, and live it. The truth is all about Jesus. To love truth is to love Jesus.

One more thing. The same week we prayed about the robbery at our church, one of the crooks turned himself in to the police.

The truth shall set him free.

------ # & ! $ # + % ----

Talking Points

1. The next time your friends claim that opposites can both be true, ask them if the opposite of their claim is also true.

Be ready for puzzled looks: "So, if you're saying that something and its opposite can both be true, then you'd have to agree that something and its opposite can't both be true, right?" If they argue with you, deny you said anything—they have no basis to disagree.

2. Try creating an endless loop of "That's true for you but not for me" argumentation.

It might sound like this:

> YOU: Jesus died for your sins, and wants to bring you to God and to heaven, too.
> YOUR FRIEND: Well, that might be true for you, but it's not true for me.
> YOU: No, that's true for you, but it's not true for me.
> YOUR FRIEND: Huh?

Most of your friends won't get the "loop" idea, but it's worth a try. When they're totally frustrated ask them...

3. Are you saying that there are no truths that are true for everybody?

If they say yes, then ask, "But didn't you just state a truth that's true for everybody?" If they say no—allowing that some truths might be true for everybody—ask them which ones. Ask them how to tell the difference between absolute and relative truths.

You can also probe their thinking with questions like: "Let's say that an engineer is calculating roof trusses for an elementary school. Should she base her calculations on a) what's true for her, or b) absolute truths for all engineers?" Show them the absurdity of the "That's true for you but not for me" argument and how nobody really lives that way.

Your point is not that you can prove the Bible or Jesus or Christianity the same way a scientist can prove the atomic weight of barium. You can't. Instead, your point is to create a little humility by gently helping your friends notice their own inconsistencies.

4. Bring the discussion back to Jesus.

It's not your goal to be right. It's your goal to point others to the best person and best friend you've ever known: Jesus. Even if you have to say, "I'm not sure I can answer all your questions about truth," you can also say, "But I do know that Jesus said, 'I am the truth' and that he loved you enough to give his life for you. He wants you and he cares about you."

------ # & ! $ # + % ----

CLICK IT: www.FourLetterWords.org/true

SCAN IT:

powered by BWSCAN.com

"Therefore, Lord... we believe that you are something than which nothing greater can be thought."[1]

ST. ANSELM (A.D. 1033 – 1109)

Touchy Ideas

1. Faith is a valid way of knowing stuff.
2. Everybody has faith—it's just not always in true things.
3. Faith in a falsehood is invalid faith.
4. Many scientific or rational objections to Christianity are based more on faith than on science or logic.
5. If faith is the weak link in the Christian chain of knowing, then it's the weak link in every chain.

Touchy Scriptures

1. But these are written that you may believe that Jesus is the Christ, the Son of God, and that believing you may have life in His name. (John 20:31)
2. These things I have written to you who believe in the name of the Son of God, that you may know that you have eternal life, and that you may continue to believe in the name of the Son of God. (1 John 5:13)

3. Therefore concerning the eating of things offered to idols, we know that an idol is nothing in the world, and that there is no other God but one. (1 Corinthians 8:4)

------ # & ! $ # + % ----

How Do You Know?

For Jews request a sign, and Greeks seek after wisdom; but we preach Christ crucified, to the Jews a stumbling block and to the Greeks foolishness, but to those who are called, both Jews and Greeks, Christ the power of God and the wisdom of God.
1 Corinthians 1:22-24

A T THE HEIGHT OF MY PERSONAL conflict with evolution, I had a pretty deep cafeteria talk with Dave, a high school friend. He was one of my smartest friends—now a Ph.D. biology professor at a major American university. He was also one of my most non-religious friends. He wasn't anti-religious; he treated my faith and me with respect. He just didn't care much about Jesus or the Bible.

Our most memorable lunch debate revolved around evolution. I ate standard public-school cafeteria fare: leathery hamburger, no cheese, extra ketchup, and fries. Plus coleslaw I was forced to take but refused to eat. Dave ate a cheeseburger.

He nailed me with the argument that he had science on his side, but I only had faith. I was stumped. Faith vs. Science seemed like an unfair fight, with Faith as the 98-pound weakling. Dave struck all the standard evolutionary blows: the fossil record, natural selection, the geological record, there's no way Noah's flood could have happened, the scientific consensus. What made our debate extra-painful was that he was so *nice* about it. I was doomed. Until I asked the Question.

The Question redefined our whole conversation. I kept asking it over and over. I asked the Question so often that, by the end of lunch, Dave admitted that my faith in Christ wasn't such a weak thing after all. What was the Question that broke through to him?

"How do you know?"

No matter what he told me about evolution, I just asked, "How do you know?" Not how do other people know, or how do scientists know, or how do mathematicians know, but how do you personally know what you know?

I kept asking until he grinned a sly smile and conceded, "Through faith."

Making Peace with Faith

I've made peace with faith. I used to think it was something I had to hide, like a flaw in the system. I believed in a Creator God by faith, but couldn't prove Him to my friends or myself. So I lived with a brittle confidence, nervous that the sheer weight of logic and science would eventually shatter my sheltered Christian cubicle.

As the third film in the *Indiana Jones* franchise races toward its climax, Indy, while searching for the Holy Grail, steps into a gaping chasm toward certain death. He takes this step of faith, *against* all logic and evidence, only to find his foot planted on an invisible bridge.

In that scene, faith and rationality oppose each other, as if faith goes hand in hand with intellectual suicide.

That was precisely my struggle. I was ready for faith, but couldn't bring myself to throw my intellect off the bus. I wanted both, but didn't think I could have both.

Then I discovered there was more faith in the world than dirt, and that everything anybody knew, they came to know at least partly through faith. I'm not calling faith "dirt." I'm just saying that, just as there's a whole lot of dirt in the world, there's a whole lot of faith—more than most of us realize. If you're going to badmouth faith as a weak link in the Christian chain of knowing, then you have to admit it's in every chain—modern, postmodern, scientific, religious, empirical, rational, or mathematical. We're all passengers on the same ship of faith.

Before you send me off for therapy, think with me.

The Shape of the Moon

Consider the shape of the moon. Is it round like a pancake or round like a ball? Obviously like a ball. A sphere.

Here's where I ask you the Question: *How do you know?*

You have only three conceivable ways of knowing this tidbit of information. You might not like the third one, and the first two don't work the way you'd expect.

The First Way: Empiricism

One way to discover the shape of the moon is to fly there and check it yourself. Astronauts have done that, of course. So we know conclusively from human experience that the moon is more like a sphere than a pancake.

Philosophers call this experiential kind of knowing *empiricism*. It's also called the "empirical method" and the "scientific method." Empiricism boils down to your five senses. What you see, hear, touch, taste, and feel is what you know. Philosophers like John Locke argued that our minds were blank slates—he said it in Latin, *tabula rasa,* think "erased markerboards"—until we built truth upon truth through our senses.

In fact, sixteenth-century Scottish philosopher, David Hume, taught that all knowledge enters our mind through the gate of our senses. And Nietzsche declared, "All credibility, all good conscience, all evidence of truth come only from the senses."[2]

This is why science is built on the senses: observation, experimentation, and replication. Until science has directly observed a phenomenon—say the evolution of one species into another—its conclusions remain tentative and are called *theories,* not facts.

The empirical method helped lift society out of the Dark Ages. Every vaccine you've received is based on observation, experimentation, and replication. The electricity that lights up your computer screen is a product of science. So are safe drinking water and air conditioning. Thank God for the empirical method.

So, when we ask how we know the moon is round like a ball, the answer is simple: we know it empirically. The astronauts who went there told us so.

You might argue, "Hey, I like the empirical method. You said it wouldn't work the way I'd expect." I know, I know. Give me a few more paragraphs till I devastate you, okay? I'll be gentle.

A voice from the past, maybe Ptolemy or Eratosthenes, might shout forward through the corridors of time, "Attention twenty-first century people: we figured out that the moon was a sphere long before spaceships went there." How did they do it?

Simple. They did the math.

The Second Way: Rationalism

So now you're on my side, thinking, "You're right. I don't like how this option works; I hate math." See? Soon you'll be sprinting in my direction.

Mathematics is the tip of a gigantic iceberg of knowledge called *rationalism*. We can also call it logic, reason, or deductive reasoning. Rationalism suggests that we acquire knowledge by combining one truth with another truth and coming up with new truths. Major premise plus minor premise equals new conclusion. That new conclusion can then serve as a new premise in an endless quest for new conclusions.

Almost 200 years ago, Georg Hegel threw a major pie in what has become philosophy's longest-running food fight when he declared,

> What is rational is actual and what is actual is rational. On this conviction the plain man, like the philosopher, takes his stand, and from it, philosophy starts in its study of the universe of mind as well as the universe of nature.[3]

Empiricists squared off against rationalists. They asked where rationalists got their very first truth—the mother of all truths—if not from their five senses, which would make them empiricists. Rationalists shot back that there are certain self-evident truths that get the ball rolling. Like the law of identity which says $a = a$. It's a good starting point, so let's just assume it's true, and keep moving.

Rationalists like Socrates, Plato, and Descartes believed that we know what we know because we deduced it logically from self-evident starting points.

As a natural-born geek, I have a hard time curbing my enthusiasm for rationalism. I love the vast, interior world of the mind. The idea of endlessly combining truths to form new ones feels like fun. Sorry, I can't help it.

Rationalism gave us math, which gave us engineers, which gave us football stadiums, which gave us many exciting hours of cheering for our favorite teams.

It also saved a lot of time. If rationalism and mathematics can show that the earth is pretty much a sphere, and that the sun is pretty much a sphere, you can safely infer that most round-looking celestial objects are spheres instead of pancakes, including the moon. It's efficient that way.

Without using these terms, my high school friend, Dave, pointed the big guns of empiricism and rationalism against my pea-shooter-sized faith.

What neither of us realized was that God majors in using pea-sized projectiles to topple giants.

The Third Way: Faith

When I was maybe six or seven, I asked my older cousin Linda why we had day and night. She held a bright red tomato next to a nearby table lamp. She dug her fingernail into the tomato to dent the skin. Then she said the lamp was like the sun, the tomato was like the earth, and we lived by the dent. She spun the tomato around and explained how the earth spins around. When our side of earth faced the sun, it was day. When it faced away from the sun, it was night.

I was skeptical. I pointed out that it was still light on the backside of the tomato and asked how come we don't fall off the fingernail dent. It took some doing, but she convinced me. She seemed to know what she was talking about.

Odds are strong that the way you learned that the moon is spherical is the same way I learned about day and night: *somebody else told you and you believed.*

Odds are also strong that most of what you know you came to know the same way. An older cousin or a teacher or a parent or a pastor spoke with authority and you believed. Faith is not simply an anti-intellectual step into nothingness, it is first and foremost *confidence in an authority.*

Even for scientific stuff. That's why I kept asking Dave the Question.

Dave said, "There's a fossil record, and it shows how life became more complex over time."

I said, "How do you know?"

He said, "Well, scientists have dug this stuff up and they've described it."

I said, "How do you know?"

He said, "Well, I read about it."

I said, "Well, I read about a Creator God."

Neither Dave nor I had a direct experience of cosmic origins. We both accepted the testimony of an authority. Our parents or teachers or textbooks or preachers told us stuff, and we believed them.

We have a word for this.

Faith.

We both had faith; we just confided it in different authorities.

I know a great many things by faith. I know that the moon is a sphere, that New Zealand is an island in the south-west Pacific, that peanuts grow underground, that coffee beans grow on trees instead of accrete on cave walls as crystals, that a long time ago a volcano wiped out Pompeii, and that the Baltimore Orioles play in Camden Yards.

Others can make those claims first hand. I can't. Other people have an empirical and/or rational basis for knowing that stuff. I don't. I take their word for it. I know all of that and so much more by faith.

You might be silently shouting—"Hey smart guy, we have pictures and eyewitness testimony and evidence that the moon's a sphere. It's not just faith!"

Nice try. Haven't you heard of *Photoshop*? You still have to take a leap of faith to believe the truthfulness of that kind of evidence. Faith is confidence in someone else's testimony.

Most of what we know, we know by faith, and if you're going to condemn Christians for basing their system on faith, shouldn't you be fair and hold yourself to the same standard—thus condemning a whole lot of what you know and how you came to know it? Perhaps including evolution, or the denial of miracles, or the Big Bang?

That's how I made peace with faith. Partly. It gets deeper.

More Faith than Dirt

You might argue, "You're right in that I don't like the third way (faith), though I grudgingly agree that a lot of what's in my head got there by faith. But I'm perfectly fine with the first two. In fact, I'd say there's more empiricism than faith. And there's more rationalism than faith. And even if I don't know stuff directly, there's still more empirical data and rational calculation to support my worldview instead of yours. After all, if I really wanted to prove the moon's a sphere, I could fly up there and take a look—but how are you going to prove Jesus is God? I still have science and logic on my side—you're stuck with measly faith."

Okay. Let's chip away at that confidence right now.

The Mother of all Knowledge

I don't want to give the impression that empiricism, rationalism, and faith are mutually exclusive categories, like aliens from three different planets who can't communicate with each other. No. The three are much more like relatives at a coffee shop, interacting, sharing biscotti, and laughing at each other's jokes.

Nor am I saying that Christianity sacrifices logic or science. Not at all. It embraces both. Rightly respected, faith, reason, and experience get along famously.

But, when you picture these relatives at the table, you should picture two children and a mom. They're not equals. I would like to make the case the Faith is the mother of the other two.

During the middle of my slow-motion, seven-year college program, I thought a lot about what I believed. I began to suspect an argument based on faith as the weakest argument of all. Sometimes a part of me still thinks that way.

So I wrote another life-changing term paper. This one was on Epistemology, which is the philosophical inquiry into how we know stuff, which is exactly what we've been talking about since the beginning of this chapter. The class was called Introduction to Philosophy. The giant lecture hall held about two hundred students, so I went unnoticed.

Until I wrote an epistemological term paper the teacher's aide really liked. All I did was suggest that rationalism and empiricism both begin with a leap of faith. Think of the hackles that would raise! Hardcore scientists, brilliant logicians, dedicated atheists, convinced evolutionists, and my friend, Dave, having to admit their chains of knowledge dangled from a link of faith. Hah!

Here's how someone might make that case.

Empiricism and Faith

Empiricism boils down to the five senses. Even as a kid you probably had discussions wondering if what you see and feel is real. How do you know that you're not just imagining everything? That your whole life isn't a dream? Or a figment of God's colorful imagination? Or a scene from *The Matrix* or *Inception?* Or a detailed fantasy telepathically inserted into your brain? How do you know that what your senses tell you is an accurate depiction of a universe that really exists outside your brain?

Answer: you don't know, at least not through evidence. You *assume* that your five senses work, and then you build your empirical empire upon that assumption. Philosophers call that assumption *a priori* knowledge. Physicist and cosmologist Dr. Paul Davies, a professor at Arizona State University, calls it faith. In his *New York Times* article, "Taking Science on Faith", he wrote,

> Over the years I have often asked my physicist colleagues why the laws of physics are what they are. The answers vary from "that's not a scientific question" to "nobody knows." The favorite reply is, "There is no reason they are what they are — they just are." The idea that the laws exist reasonlessly is deeply anti-rational.... [U]ntil science comes up with a testable theory of the laws of the universe, its claim to be free of faith is manifestly bogus.[4]

Step one in the vast empire called empiricism is faith—faith in your observations and in your senses. Don't get me wrong; I'm not knocking it. I'm pro-faith. I'm just pointing it out.

But if we're going to knock Christians for taking their leap of faith, isn't it only fair that we use the same standard to knock scientists and empiricists and Starbucks baristas and students and teachers and politicians and modernists and postmodernists and truck drivers and mechanics and agnostics and ourselves and pretty much everybody for taking the same leap?

What I wrote in my paper was that the whole system of empiricism rests on a foundation of faith; you can't avoid it. If you consider faith a corrosive element, then look carefully at your own scientific system for rust.

"Nice job!" commented the teacher's assistant.

Rationalism and Faith

I made the same argument with rationalism, though it was easier. Because rationalists admit a set of unproven presuppositions called Postulates (or Axioms). Not only are they unproven, they are unprovable. Which to me smells a whole lot like faith.

Mr. or Ms. Rationalist, I ask you, how do you know that $a = a$? Can you prove it?

Even a basic algebra text acknowledges that mathematics rests on unprovable assumptions. Here's how Wikipedia explains it:

> In traditional logic, an axiom or postulate is a proposition that is not proved or demonstrated but considered to be either self-evident, or subject to necessary decision. Therefore, its truth is taken for granted, and serves as a starting point for deducing and inferring other (theory dependent) truths.[5]

Not proven. Taken for granted.

Sounds like faith.

Faith is trust in an authority: for empiricism, the authority is our senses. For rationalism, the authority is our postulates—the logical concepts that get the rational ball rolling. For Christianity, the authority is Jesus and his Word.

EVERY SYSTEM RESTS ON FAITH

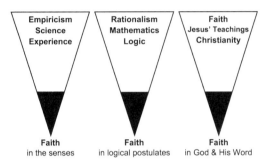

In my paper I wrote that not only does the empirical method rest squarely on a foundation of faith, but so does rationalism. The three great systems of thought are like inverted pyramids, resting massive edifices of knowledge on a tiny tip of faith.

Yet, even with all this faith, we still have a sense of certainty and confidence in what we know. We would argue with a flat-moon theorist just as we would argue with a scientist from the past who put the earth at the center of the solar system. We're confident enough about most stuff to fight for it. Even though it rests on faith.

I'm just saying that faith and confidence go hand in hand; they're not opposites. That's why I can be so confident Jesus is my Savior and that I find life's meaning in him, and not in an arrogant way. Why should the fact that my system rests on faith undercut my confidence in Christ? If every system rests on faith, why should I be any less confident in Christ Jesus' forgiveness and love than a scientist is confident in her evolution or a rationalist in his postulates?

We're just pinning our faith to different authorities. That's not to say that Christianity is irrational or non-experiential. For me, it is supremely rational—it makes more sense than any other world-view—even though I don't have answers for all my doubts. It's supremely experiential, too. God seems real to me. Jesus is precious to me. In my life, faith joins hands with reason and experience and walks them across the busy street called life.

People who are skeptical about Christianity aren't really skeptical about faith; after all, they use faith every moment of every day.

They're skeptical of our authority: the Bible. Now, that's a different conversation, isn't it?

Anyhow, that's how I made peace with Faith. Yeah... I'm a Christian and my system is built on faith. I admit it.

Do you?

By the way, Dave, my brilliant friend and a professor of biology, is now also one of the most devoted followers of Jesus I know. Maybe faith isn't intellectual suicide after all.

------ # & ! $ # + % ----

Talking Points

1. Ask the Question... relentlessly.

Ask, "How do you know?" When skeptics question your faith, question theirs. Be polite but insistent. Your goal is to help them see that their system—whatever it may be—balances nervously on faith. Make it very personal, too. How do they personally know that there is no God, or that life evolved, or that Jesus never rose from the dead? What is their evidence, and how do they know it's true? Eventually, they'll come to confess that they know what they know by faith.

2. Stay between the lines: be confident but not cocky and be humble but not wimpy.

It's okay to know that you're saved, to know that you have eternal life, to know that Jesus is your Savior, to know that Jesus is God, and to know that there is no Savior but him. You know these things by faith—and by the end of this book you'll know why that faith is a reasonable one. Don't wimp out and apologize for Jesus. The Bible says, "These things I have written to you who believe in the name of the Son of God, that you may know that you have eternal life, and that you may continue to believe in the name of the Son of God" (1 John 5:13).

3. Don't be intimidated by brainiacs.

Some of the smartest people in history have been committed Christians.

Start with Jesus and Paul. Move on to Augustine, Anselm and Aquinas. Jump ahead to Luther and Calvin. Don't forget C.S. Lewis. Add Francis Collins, the scientist who led the human genome project, and left his atheism behind when he encountered Jesus through reading *Mere Christianity.*[6] Really smart Christians, all. We have two thousand years of intellectual heavyweights taking their stand on faith in Christ. You'd have to radically revise history to question the collective intelligence of global Christianity. That doesn't mean we're perfect. It's just to say that Jesus' invitation has always appealed to the brainiest among us.

4. Personalize the quest.

Don't let the conversation be about naked ideas—let it be about knowing God through Jesus. If we just know stuff about a person, we're like star-struck fans of the latest celebrity. But if that knowledge leads us into a friendship or community with the person, it has served its purpose.

All truth is God's truth. That means everything we know—whether through reason, experience, or faith—becomes God's invitation to join in community with him:

> We are telling you about what we ourselves have actually seen and heard, so that you may have fellowship [community] with us. And our fellowship [community] is with the Father and with his Son, Jesus Christ. (1 John 1:3, NLT)

It's pretty wild to picture ourselves in community with God. You'll never prove God or Jesus or the Bible or even the Christian worldview by your arguments. The best you can do is to soften some objections and generate some humility in those who resist Jesus' love. But don't lose sight of that love, and of the invitation Jesus has asked you to deliver—into the mystery of community with the Father and Son through the Spirit.

------ # & ! $ # + % ----

CLICK IT: www.FourLetterWords.org/know

SCAN IT:

powered by SWSCAN.com

CHAPTER 4

We wonder, ever wonder, why we find us here!
Has some Vast Imbecility,
Mighty to build and blend
But impotent to tend,
Framed us in jest, and left us now to hazardry?
THOMAS HARDY (RELIGIOUS SKEPTIC, 1840-1928)

------ # & ! $ # + % ----

Touchy Ideas

1. God can stop pain but he doesn't.
2. Even though he doesn't stop it, his love never flickers.

Touchy Scriptures

1. How long shall I take counsel in my soul, Having sorrow in my heart daily? How long will my enemy be exalted over me? (Psalm 13:2)

2. How long, LORD? Will You hide Yourself forever? Will Your wrath burn like fire? (Psalm 89:46)

3. O LORD, do not rebuke me in your anger or discipline me in your rage. Have compassion on me, LORD, for I am weak. Heal me, LORD, for my body is in agony. I am sick at heart. How long, O LORD, until you restore me? (Psalm 6:1-3, NLT)

4. 2 O LORD, how long shall I cry, And You will not hear? Even cry out to You, "Violence!" And You will not save. 3 Why do You

show me iniquity, And cause me to see trouble? For plundering and violence are before me; There is strife, and contention arises. (Habakkuk 1:2, 3)

------ # & ! $ # + % ----

A WOMAN SITS IN THE EXAMINATION room unable to wrap her mind around the news. Yes, the lump is cancer. The numbness that grips her soul strangles even the faintest cry.

A businessman sits at his computer reviewing the numbers again. The room is cold, yet sweat stains his shirt. He will lose his company, and with it the financial security he's built up for a lifetime.

A father holds his daughter close as the girl weeps that she has no date for the prom because she's "ugly." Her father sees only beauty. Something inside him aches to hurt the boys who hurt his girl.

A woman wraps her arms around herself in a darkened room. They told her these things happen and it is nature's way of taking care of mistakes. But her child wasn't a mistake. She can't imagine walking back into her world without the little one whose presence she felt and whose heartbeat she had seen and heard through ultrasound.

A boy sits at his desk. He is supposed to be doing homework, but he can't concentrate. His mind wonders how any person can do the things that have been done to him. He feels violated and guilty. He allows a lone tear to run down his face.

From the depths of our souls, from the deepest parts of our brains, a haunting question arises: *God, where are you? If you love me, how can you let me hurt so much?*

The Problem of Pain

My history professor in seminary suggested the problem of pain keeps more people away from God than any other. When he said it, I was skeptical. Most of my friends were stuck on scientific or logical objections, not pain.

But we were bulletproof twenty-somethings.

Then life happened. A friend broke his back: paralyzed for life. Someone's son killed himself. A much prayed-for pregnancy ended in miscarriage. The more we asked why, the more we turned a suspicious eye toward God.

In the oldest book in the Bible, a man named Job suffered so much, he accused God of painting a bull's-eye on his back: "Have I sinned? What have I done to You, O watcher of men? Why have You set me as Your target, So that I am a burden to myself?" (Job 7:20).

Job, like anybody who's lived much, crashed into the problem of pain, and questioned God over it.

I think God welcomes our questions, like we welcome a call from an old friend. It's just that sometimes he doesn't answer out loud. I don't know why. It probably has something to do with, a) the relative sizes of our brains, and, b) his fondness for stretching our faith. Most of the time, he doesn't even acknowledge that he heard our questions. Still, he loves our company and he never resents our questions.

The problem arises when we quit questioning him. We can easily let the problem of pain drive a wedge between us and God, and just leave the wedge there, like a thorn. First, it's painful and swollen. Then it gets infected. Then it scars over. Then it grows numb. Then we kick God to the curb, deciding he's irrelevant.

That's when our soul's "ouch" becomes a four letter word against God.

The Problem Stated

One of the oldest philosophical statements of the problem comes from a Greek philosopher named Epicurus (341-270 B.C.). He wrote,

> God either wants to eliminate bad things and cannot,
> or can but does not want to, or neither
> wishes to nor can, or both wants to and
> can.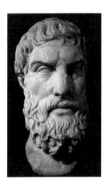
> If he wants to and cannot, he is weak—
> and this does not apply to God.
> If he can but does not want to, then he
> is spiteful—which is equally foreign to
> God's nature.
> If he neither wants to nor can, he is both
> weak and spiteful and so not a god.
> If he wants to and can, which is the only thing fitting
> for a god, where then do bad things come from? Or
> why does he not eliminate them?[1,2]

Epicurus never solved this problem; he just lived with it. A Christian philosopher, named Lactantius, said that Epicurus' goal was to make people give up the delusion that god cares about them.[3]

Philosophers call Epicurus' statement the "Inconsistent Triad." It involves three ideas that some say can't all be true: 1) The existence of evil. 2) An all-good God. 3) An all-powerful God. Whenever we give voice to the problem of pain, we're suggesting that at least one corner of the triangle has taken a break.

The Inconsistent Triad poses such a great problem that John Stott, one of our generation's most knowledgeable Christian teachers, said, "The fact of suffering undoubtedly constitutes the single greatest challenge to the Christian faith."[4] My own experience as a follower of Jesus and a pastor confirms this: the problem of pain is a huge stumbling block for people seeking God. We'll spend two chapters thinking it through.

The technical name for this topic is *theodicy*. We're "justifying" God for permitting the problem of pain and the existence of evil. The thought of justifying God makes me jittery—like I sent him to the principal's office to explain himself—when I know deep inside that I need to explain myself to him. That's one of the beautiful things about God: he can humble himself without losing himself. He lets low life-forms like me put him on trial.

```
===================================
```
theodicy. the*od"i*cy\, n. [...fr. Gr. *theos*, God + *dikaios*, **right, justice...] A vindication of the justice of God in ordaining or permitting natural and moral evil.**[5]
```
===================================
```

Four main theodicies have captivated the world's imagination across the millennia: Animism, Naturalism, Monism, and Christianity. (Other monotheistic religions, like Islam and Judaism, offer their own spin on these themes, so we won't deal directly with them.)

Don't get spooked by the technical names; I'll bet it's stuff you've already thought of. You'll most likely find yourself in one of these camps—perhaps with variations. For me, the most plausible and coherent theodicy is the one offered by historic, biblical Christianity. I'd like to show you why. We'll cover Animism and Naturalism in this chapter, and save Monism and Christianity for the next.

The Theodicy of Animism and Idol Worship

Animism sees intelligent spirits lurking behind the forces of nature, including pain. So, you didn't trip over a rock, the spirit of the rock made you trip. And it wasn't just hurricanes that rampaged across the Gulf of Mexico, it was the spirits of the hurricane. Ditto for idol worship. Each idol contains one or more spirits that impact everyday life.

I'm writing this chapter fresh off a visit to Gabon, a country in West Africa. Our church family supports a hospital there, along with a surgical school, nursing school, midwife school, eye clinic, dental clinic, and AIDS clinic.

The head surgeon explained that village life was rooted in animism. People believed they got sick because somebody cast a spell on them or wished them ill, and the spirits made it happen. Old-timers suspected an enemy's revenge behind virtually everything that went wrong, because the enemy sent a bad spirit against them. This motivated the victim to get even, which meant having to figure out who wished him ill. Enter the witch doctor, who made the suspects drink toxic stew. If you got sick, you must be guilty. Never mind that you were basically drinking filth mixed with poison, the spirits knew how to "out" the perpetrator.

This led to endless rounds of injury, accusation, and revenge. Even if the victim couldn't take revenge on you, he'd make sure his children would take revenge on your children.

Animism and idol worship produce fear. Growing up, I heard many times that missionaries shouldn't bother less-developed cultures. We shouldn't inflict our ways on them, because they're happy without our conveniences, our beliefs, and our technology.

I believed this view during my young twenties. I worried about missionaries spoiling happy tribes by barging in with the "westernized" message of Jesus.

Then I heard a missionary doctor (a different one) explain that the idea tribal people are happy in their pristine isolation is a myth. Most tribal people are not happy, he said. They live in deep fear. They fear spirits of the water, the trees, the lightning, the thunder, and the tribes downriver. Other missionaries have confirmed this for me. Animism and idol worship make people afraid of almost everything most of the time.

This makes sense to me: if the gods themselves are crazy, then raise the shields and tiptoe on eggshells.

You don't have to travel to the jungles of Africa to find animism. I found it in Florence, Italy, on a crowded bus. It was standing room only and we were drenched with sweat. There was no air conditioning, and for some reason, all the windows were closed. My shirt was plastered to my body.

So I did what any sweat-soaked activist would do: I reached across some seated passengers, and flung open a window.

That wasn't smart.

A withered lady dressed in black yelled at me. She cursed me, actually, *in Italiano*, which I don't understand. My Italian-speaking friend, Pietro, said, "Bill, she wants you to close the window." I was baffled. Pietro continued, "She's superstitious; she thinks a draft is an evil spirit."

I closed the window, feeling very much a victim of the spirits that day.

The Bible's View of Animism and Idol Worship

Converted idol worshippers packed the early churches: "... you turned to God from idols to serve the living and true God (1 Thessalonians 1:9). I guess that makes idols—every one of them—dead and false gods. There was not much room for pluralism in St. Paul's mind.

Bible people rubbed shoulders with animists every day. Unfortunately, animism was contagious. The writers of the Bible suspected the human carnage it would leave in its wake, so they commanded God's followers to steer clear. That didn't stop them.

If spirits cause my pain, then I must influence, manipulate, cajole, or bribe them to deliver their pain elsewhere—let's say to you. Sometimes, this effort turns violent. Throughout history, tribal religions have practiced human sacrifice to placate the spirits. Women and children were most at risk.

They still are.

Others influenced the gods through ritualized sex acts. Some ancient religions, like the Gnostic cults and the idol worship of Canaan, reasoned that acts of fertility on earth could stimulate acts of fertility in heaven which would, in turn, uh—fertilize the crops. Even God's own people were sucked into this. So God sent prophets to tell them:

- Do not give any of your children as a sacrifice to Molech, for you must not profane the name of your God. I am the LORD. (Leviticus 18:21, NLT).

- Are there any among the idols of the nations that can cause rain? Or can the heavens give showers? Are You not He, O LORD our God? Therefore we will wait for You, Since You have made all these. (Jeremiah 14:22).

Other idol worshippers, in their quest to control the spirits, cut themselves with knives "till the blood gushed out" (1 Kings 18:28). Egyptian priests entombed living slaves with their dead pharaohs. The wives of tribal chiefs were often buried alive with their husbands. Infants writhed in agony on the red-hot hands of super-heated idols. Cannibals ate their conquered enemies.

No one ever accused the spirits of playing nice.

MOLECH (JER. 32:35)

These worldviews prove that *ideas have consequences.* It's like boarding a train. When you hop on board animism—or any worldview—you have to ride it to its destination. So it makes sense to study the destination before you buy the ticket, don't you think?

If you buy into the ideas that, a) the problem of pain is a function of spirits who are unpredictable or crazy, and; b) they can be manipulated by sacrificing ourselves and others, and; c) if you do it right, you can send the problem of pain downstream to the next tribe, then, you have to accept the consequences of those ideas.

Historically, those consequences have been nightmarish: human sacrifice, self-mutilation, vengeance-hungry cultures, cannibalism, promiscuity, violence toward women and children, slavery, oppression, and all-pervasive fear. Yes, Christians have inflicted their share of inhumanity across the globe, and for it, I grieve and apologize. But those evils are the exception, not the rule. They flow, not from biblical Christianity, but from a distortion of it.

But the evils that follow animism and idol worship are the rule, not the exception, and they flow logically from its premises. Ideas have consequences.

Animism and Idol Worship: A Loving Critique

1. Animism and idol worship make us pawns in an unpredictable universe. We're at the mercy of capricious gods and whimsical spirits. They cause the problem of pain. These spirits demean human dignity and make us scramble to placate them.

2. Animism and idol worship deflect the problem of pain by shifting the pain to others. Vengeance, human sacrifice, cannibalism, slavery, inter-tribal hatred, and war: these are some of the outgrowths of animism.

3. Animism and idol worship offer no solution to the problem of pain. No ultimate healing. No balancing the scales of justice. Pain wins in the end.

I'm not suggesting that animism and idol worship attract only barbarous infidels. People reared in these beliefs can make for kind-hearted neighbors and socially conscious civic leaders. My goal is to probe these beliefs for inconsistencies, to trace out their conclusions, and then to ask you to make up your own mind. Is animism a plausible worldview for today? Does its solution (or non-solution) to the problem of pain work for you? Does it give you an *aha!* moment that makes sense of your losses? Does it heal broken hearts?

If animism doesn't work for you, you can always test-drive a second widely-held worldview called naturalism.

The Theodicy of Naturalism

Construction on the *Biosphere* experiment began in 1967 to see if a self-contained ecosystem could sustain life indefinitely. Completed in 1991, it covers about two and a half football fields. It was a completely closed system. In its heyday, the Biosphere boasted a rainforest, an 850-square meter mini-ocean, a desert, farmland, recycling systems, and human living quarters. Its first occupants, eight researchers, spent two years locked inside the airtight structure.[6]

The Biosphere became their world. Nothing went in and nothing went out, not even air. The rainforest and farm produced oxygen, purified the air and water, recycled waste, and provided all the food the occupants needed. The Biosphere let scientists gather ecological data on a larger scale than they ever could before. Today, the Biosphere has outlived most of its scientific purposes and remains open for tours.

To committed naturalists, the cosmos is a massive biosphere. It is a closed system with no outside input—not from spirits, not from angels, and not from God. There is nothing outside the cosmos: nothing feeds into it, nothing sustains it, and nothing transcends it.

Contrast that with my son's fish tank. From Pip's perspective (the fish), every day the sky opens and a hand dispenses food flakes. I wonder what Pip thinks of the hand. It must look like God to him. Without regular water changes, cleanup, and food flakes from the hand, the tank turns toxic and Pip goes belly-up. The fish tank is an open system. It requires an outside hand to sustain it. The hand transcends the tank.

The closed Biosphere, without outside input, represents *naturalism*. The open fish tank, with regular outside input, represents *supernaturalism*.

Scientists have been poking each other in the eye over these worldviews since at least five centuries before Christ. A Greek philosopher, Thales of Miletus, argued that, even though there are

gods, we should still look for nature-based explanations of the world before we blame or credit a god.[7]

You might be surprised to know it was Christians who ran with Thales' argument. During the Renaissance, Christian leaders reasoned we should seek natural explanations before we turned to supernatural ones. The direct hand of God, they argued, didn't cause every eclipse, volcanic eruption, or plague. God's laws of nature were sufficient to explain much of what happened.

This view appeals to me, even though I don't think it allows enough room for God's shepherding of the cosmos. It allowed for the supernatural intervention of God in rare cases (a.k.a. miracles) while it also recognized God's hand in setting up the natural laws of the cosmos to begin with.

That's why, when my son needed surgery, we went to the hospital, a natural solution, and prayed for healing, a supernatural solution.

Metaphysical naturalism, however, kissed God goodbye and closed off the cosmic system to him once for all. *Deists,* like Benjamin Franklin, believed God might have created the cosmos, but had little to do with it anymore. *Atheists,* like Richard Dawkins, believe there is not now, and never was, a supernatural realm to begin with. So no God, devil, angels, demons, or Creator. No prayer. No human soul or spirit. No afterlife. No heaven, or hell, miracles, or eternity. Nothing outside nature's realm at all. Our planet wanders through its own massive biosphere—a closed system with nothing outside it, and no conscious mind guiding it from the inside.

Dawkins pokes fun at the idea of a Creator, which he compares to a "watchmaker:"

> All appearances to the contrary, the only watchmaker in nature is the blind forces of physics, albeit deployed in a very special way. A true watchmaker has foresight: he designs his cogs and springs, and plans their interconnections, with a future purpose in his mind's eye. Natural selection... has no purpose in mind. It has no mind and no mind's eye. It does not plan for the future. It has no vision, no foresight, no sight at all. If it can be said to play the role of watchmaker in nature, it is the blind watchmaker.[8]

What does naturalism say about the problem of pain? It says nothing, because there is no "problem" of pain. The impersonal laws of nature have their way with us, and that's it. We're stuck in a cosmic machine that churns out random life forms and indiscriminate suffering and there is no point to it other than what we make up. Your soul's "ouch" is nothing more than the survival instinct at work—a complex interaction of matter and energy. Even your joys and the things you celebrate are just "fortunate" chemical reactions we could recreate in a lab if we had the technology. The problem of pain is, at root, chemical.

Maybe that's why we swallow so many chemicals to solve it.

The Bible's View of Naturalism

The Bible presents a *supernatural* worldview. God created the cosmos and keeps it humming. He is greater than it but involved with it. Transcendent yet immanent, to use the theological terms.

The people Jesus hung out with were supernaturalists—though some had their doubts. Jesus faced down the Sadducees, a Jewish sect that denied a resurrection, angels, and an afterlife. He told them they were mistaken and didn't know the power of God (Matthew 22:23-32). The Apostle Paul almost started a riot between the Sadducees (mainly naturalists) and the Pharisees (mainly supernaturalists) when he told a Jewish council that he was on trial for his confidence in the resurrection of the dead. The Bible says, "And when he had said this, a dissension [a big fight] arose between the Pharisees and the Sadducees; and the assembly was divided. For Sadducees say that there is no resurrection—and no angel or spirit; but the Pharisees confess both" (Acts 23:7,8).

When Paul said of Jesus, "And He is before all things, and in Him all things consist," he used two technical, philosophical terms (Colossians 1:17).

The term "all things" was the technical term for the cosmos. It included the universe and everything in it. Paul dropped a philosophical bombshell when asserted that Jesus, whose sandals trod the dusty streets of Nazareth, pre-existed the cosmos. He didn't stop there, though.

He also claimed that, by Jesus, the cosmos "consists." In those days, Stoic and Platonic philosophers used this verb *(sunistémi)* for the force that held the cosmos together, and kept the laws of nature intact.[9] Knowing this, St. Paul picked that same word, as if to say, "That's Jesus' job." The early Christians used the term *Pantocrator*, which means Almighty One or "Cosmic Powerhouse," to describe him.[10]

What if there is a personal being who transcends the biosphere and takes care of it? What if the cosmos is a fishbowl and the hand of God drops in moment-by-moment sustenance?

There's no way to read the Bible and come away feeling that the power that governs the universe is indifferent to the cosmos or its pain.

Naturalism and the Problem of Pain: A Loving Critique

1. Naturalism can only offer the "shark attack" solution to the problem of pain. A marauding shark does what a shark is genetically programmed to do. We might not like it, but we can't blame it, we can't argue with it, and we can't take it personally. The universe ticks away according to natural laws without God's intervention. Pain happens.

2. There is no need for theodicy because there is no God to justify. If you board the train of naturalism, be ready to give up prayer, divine comfort, divine healing, and any hope after death. Prepare, also, to give up human sacredness. Naturalism places us on the same spectrum as a light bulb—the interaction of matter and energy—without the image of God, without the sacredness of human life, and without any more inherent value than a dog or a worm.

3. What "is" is right. You can't make moral judgments against the universe any more than you can make moral judgments against a hurricane. We live in a mechanistic system, and we ourselves are molecular machines. Pain is irrelevant. Sorry.

4. Not all naturalists go here—and there are many good-hearted naturalists who do wonderful things—but *naturalism has a dark side.* It was the driving force behind Soviet and Chinese communism, responsible for the greatest mass murders in world history. Why? Because naturalism makes human life expendable. Ideas have con-

sequences, and once you define life on naturalistic grounds, you logically promote "survival of the fittest" from a biological principle to a political strategy. If winners write the history, I've got to make sure I'm a winner at all costs, right?

5. *How can you prove that the cosmos is a closed system?* Until you have explored its boundaries, how can you prove nothing exists beyond it? Isn't that a lot like Pip, the fish, insisting, "The Aquarium is all that is or ever was or ever will be"?

IT'S EASY TO TALK ABOUT PAIN IN THE ABSTRACT, like philosophers in leather armchairs, smoking pipes, more interested in ideas than in life. But the problem of pain, like a hyperactive toddler, won't stay in its chair and play nice. It turns over tables, throws a tantrum and demands our attention. If you haven't experienced deep pain yet, you will. I'm not trying to be morbid, just real.

Pain happens, count on it.

Then what? How will you fit this piece into the puzzle that is your life? Think it through, because how you solve the problem of pain determines what you do with the reality of pain when it strikes.

So far, the two options we've considered—animism and naturalism—acknowledge the existence of pain. The third option, in the next chapter, solves the problem by denying that pain exists in the first place. It sounds intriguing, but can it explain this gaping hole in my heart?

------ # & ! $ # + % ----

Talking Points

1. Challenge the myth that tribal people without God and "western" technology are happy.

There's a simple way to do this. Ask your friend if it's a good thing to introduce tribes to antibiotics, like penicillin, or simple technologies, like mosquito nets, to stem the tide of infant deaths from malaria. Not many compassionate people would argue against that.

Follow up by asking, "If we teach them *mosquitoes* carry the germs that cause malaria, won't that mess with their view that the *spirits* cause malaria? Won't antibiotics and mosquito nets put witch doctors out of business? Aren't you messing with their religion?"

There is no way to deliver tribal cultures from disease, death, and fear without putting a dent in animism. Help your friend see how animism takes the problem of pain and rubs it raw. Explain how animistic cultures need a radically new worldview if their children and children's children are going to survive.

2. Confront the inconsistencies of naturalism.

The central inconsistency is this: if there is no God, there can be no *problem* of pain. Pain exists as a function of natural selection. It warns life-forms of danger, and ensures the survival of the fittest. So why complain about pain? Why prevent it? Why alleviate it? Why should we treat pain as a problem if there is no moral reason to do so? Under naturalism, we live in a mechanistic system, and we ourselves are molecular machines. Pain is an important tool of natural selection. We should be thankful for it, except we can't because there's no one to be thankful to. When your friends hopped on board naturalism, is this where they wanted to go?

3. Acknowledge the problem of pain and the inconsistent triad.

Don't oversimplify other people's pain and how it makes them question God. There is a mystery to suffering and evil we can't understand in this lifetime, even with the Bible. Acknowledge that mystery, and make sure your friends feel your compassion before you worry about them accepting your beliefs.

------ # & ! $ # + % ----

CLICK IT: www.FourLetterWords.org/pain

SCAN IT:

powered by BWSCAN.com

I believe in the cosmos. All of us are linked to the cosmos. So nature is my god. To me, nature is sacred. Trees are my temples and forests are my cathedrals.[1]

--MIKHAIL GORBACHEV

------ # & ! $ # + % ----

Touchy Ideas

1. There is a radical difference between creation and the Creator; God is one within himself, but he is not one with nature.
2. Individuals are important.
3. Pain is the inevitable consequence of living far from God.
4. Pain is the inevitable consequence of living too close to God without proper preparation.

Touchy Scriptures

1. LORD, how long shall I cry, And You will not hear? Even cry out to You, "Violence!" And You will not save. (Habakkuk 1:2)
2. No temptation has overtaken you except such as is common to man; but God is faithful, who will not allow you to be tempted beyond what you are able, but with the temptation will also make the way of escape, that you may be able to bear it. (1 Corinthians 10:13)
3. For I know the thoughts that I think toward you, says the LORD, thoughts of peace and not of evil, to give you a future and a hope. (Jeremiah 29:11)

4. For as the heavens are higher than the earth, So are My ways higher than your ways, And My thoughts than your thoughts. (Isaiah 55:9)

------ # & ! $ # + % ----

The Theodicy of Monism

I N THE 1995 DISNEY ANIMATION, Pocahontas sings,
You think you own whatever land you land on
The earth is just a dead thing you can claim
But I know ev'ry rock and tree and mountain
Has a life, has a spirit, has a name...
The rainstorm and the river are my brothers
The heron and the otter are my friends
And we are all connected to each other
In a circle, in a hoop that never ends.[2,3]

It's a beautiful song, but don't miss its monism and its tilt toward animism. Monism, from the word for "one," teaches all is one. Monism undergirds pantheism (all is god), panentheism (god is in all), and naturalism (nature is all). Pagan religions, like Wicca, witchcraft, and Druidism, squat comfortably on the "all is one" foundation.

So do magic, sorcery, and occultism. The only way the Harry Potters of this world can work their magic is by uniting with the cosmic energy, and letting the power flow through them.

It works that way for Jedi Knights too.

All is one.

You might have heard rumors of friction between media mogul, Oprah Winfrey, and Bible-based Christians. I respect Oprah. She's a survivor and an overcomer. She has done incredible good for people and for society. She's a great role model for determination, belief in yourself, and generosity. Oprah is a good person. I admire her. But I also disagree with her, respectfully.

Oprah has made it an open secret that she no longer believes the traditional Christianity she grew up with. She's gone beyond it. In the world of O...

- Jesus is no longer the unique Son of God who died for sins once for all. He is one of many ways to God.
- Jesus' death didn't atone for sin; it set an example of self-sacrificing love.
- God is in us all. We are divine beings. All is god, and god is all.
- Jesus wasn't God who became human, he was human who became God, just as we all can.
- New age authors like Eckhart Tolle, Eric Butterworth, Gary Zukav, and Deepak Chopra influence Oprah more than the Bible.

This isn't about knocking Oprah. It's about understanding an idea, because ideas have consequences. Some of these teachings fall within the camp of *monism*. Eric Butterworth, a minister in the (monistic) Unity Church, and an influencer of Oprah, wrote,

> Everyone must ultimately emphasize his or her own unity with God by proclaiming as Jesus did, 'I and the Father are One.' Unless we understand Jesus' concept of unity, we have lost the key to his teachings. It is the Unity Principle that explains the true meaning of 'The Christ.' Christ is not a person, but a level of the particularization of God

into the person, the focal point through which all the attributes of God are poured out into livingness.[4]

Oprah endorses Butterworth on his website.

I get why people slide toward monism. It's appealing to think of the interconnectedness of all things. Every particle exerts a gravitational pull on every other particle. As we walk around, our magnetic field interacts with everyone else and their fields. Monism believes our energy merges with the birds, the sky, the sea, the great beyond. We merge with the cycle of life. Very Pocahontas.

There's a beauty in that kind of thinking. I can see why Oprah and so many societies through the ages have believed it.

At the same time, there's something wonderful about individuality, which monism undercuts. Personhood needs individuality. I may be my brother's or sister's keeper, but I'm still me. I am a differentiated individual and I celebrate that. I celebrate your individuality, too. The monistic idea of oneness wounds that. That's why I prefer *community*—the interconnectedness of differentiated individuals—over *oneness*. The Bible does too (Acts 2:42).

One of the most beautiful mysteries of the Christian faith is that it offers a God who is solitary but not lonely. The Father, Son, and Holy Spirit—though one in essence—are three in person, and enjoy each other immensely. It is God's very essence to be relational. When God made us in his image, he made us individuals, but he wove a call toward community into our very being.

God celebrates individuality—yours, mine, and his own. He is who he is, and he is in a class by himself. So is Jesus. Monism undercuts this. That's why Christian philosopher, Francis Schaeffer, critiqued monism as "pan-everything-ism."[5]

Monism opens the door to the divine, but not to the God of the Bible. The monistic deity permeates the cosmos as salt permeates the world's oceans.

One monistic spiritualist declared, "She [the goddess Wisdom, or Sophia] is everywhere and encompasses everything: She is everything and everybody and its opposite. . . . She shows for me that there is no disunity between something and its opposite."[6]

Under monism, even opposites are one. You can kiss the law of non-contradiction goodbye. I'm not sure how that works, which, I guess is the same as saying I'm sure how that works.

If all is one and one is all, then humanity is one too. Nobody has a corner on right or wrong, on good or evil, on true or false. Instead, all is right, all is good, all is true. Humans are divine, and humans can create their own realities.

Which leads to the conclusion that...

...all religions are one.

David Steindl-Rast, a Benedictine monk, writing in the magazine *Gnosis* says: "Envision the great religious traditions arranged on the circumference of a circle. At their mystical core they all say the same thing, but with different emphasis."[7]

So if all is one, and if all people are one, and if all religions are one, then the unpardonable sin becomes splintering away from the oneness.

Like traditionally minded Christians seem to do.

Why would they do that? Because it's hard to avoid the conclusion that Jesus made exclusive claims. He said the way to God was narrow, not wide, and warned that few people find it (Matthew 7:13,14).

Monism stretches arms open wide and says, "We're all one." If you come from a monistic tradition, your faith sounds inclusive and welcoming. For Christianity to teach the exact opposite sounds narrow and bigoted. I get that. The way of monism sounds much more uplifting—until you examine monism's foundations and consider its conclusions.

For a very ugly example, convicted cult leader and mass murderer, Charles Manson (of "Helter Skelter" fame), tipped his monistic hand when he asked, "If God is one, what is bad?" Obviously, very few monists ride the train as far as Manson did, but his logic is flawless.

My conscience is bound by Scripture, which reveals a God who "has delivered us from the power of darkness and conveyed us into the kingdom of the Son of His love" (Colossians 1:13). Evidently, God doesn't see all things as one. He sees a giant disconnect between the domain of darkness and the kingdom of his beloved Son, and these opposites are irreconcilable.

Monism and the Problem of Pain

For monists, pain is a problem of perception.

"If you want to get the plain truth, be not concerned with right and wrong. The conflict between right and wrong is the sickness of the mind," said Zen Master Yun-Men.[8]

Buddhism teaches:

> There is this noble truth of dukkha [suffering]: birth is [suffering], aging is [suffering], and death is [suffering]; sorrow, lamentation, pain, grief, and despair are [suffering]; experiencing the unloved and disliked is [suffering]; separation from the beloved and satisfying is [suffering]; wanting things and not getting them is [suffering]; in short, the essence of

[suffering] is taking the five heaps to be "I" and "mine."[9,10]

In this worldview, suffering has no independent existence; it is a state of mind we must grow out of by following the Buddhist path.

We grow beyond pain by developing a passionless indifference to it. Pain is an illusion; don't believe it. That is the ultimate goal.

When sadness has invaded my life, I don't think shoving my mind into its happy place would have healed it. When my wife and I conceived our first child, we were excited and thankful to God. Some months into the pregnancy, a routine check-up gave us heartbreaking news: the little baby's heart had stopped beating.

I don't think passionless indifference would have healed our broken hearts after our miscarriage or brought me much peace when one of my childhood friends died in his early twenties from oral cancer and then another died from lupus. Those situations elicited passion from me, and I had plenty of it. My grief felt real to me. It felt right. I'm thankful I could grieve my losses and not gloss over them with passionless indifference. I feel alive that way. I feel grounded in reality.

Monism and the Bible

"Professing to be wise, they became fools, and changed the glory of the incorruptible God into an image made like corruptible man--and birds and four-footed animals and creeping things" (Romans 1:22,23).

God is not happy when we morph him with lower life forms.

God describes himself as immeasurably higher than us—in his being, thoughts, and ways (Isaiah 55:8,9). The writers of Scripture, without exception, walk a fine line: they reveal an infinite God who transcends the created order while simultaneously staying near those who trust him.

Theology experts call these truths the *transcendence* and the *immanence* of God. Both coexist in beautiful harmony on every page of Scripture.

This, ultimately, will be the solution to the problem of pain.

But, contrary to monism, we never become gods, and he only became human once, in the person of Jesus Christ. That incarnation will never be repeated—it was once for all.[11]

Oprah and other monists present Jesus as a man who understood the mysteries of monism—a man who became one with god because he understood how to work the system. He is, therefore, a man who does little more than inspire us by his example and teach us by his precepts.[12]

Scripture paints a different picture.

Jesus was the peerless, unique Son of God—that's what the phrase "only begotten" means in John 3:16. He was a one of a kind person; we can follow his steps but can never duplicate his identity. From the Bible's perspective, monists are off track. Not everything is one with everything else. We are created in the image of God, but we are not gods, and he is not us.

Monism and the Problem of Pain: A Loving Critique

1. Monism erodes human dignity.

It places us on par with rocks and lizards and fluffy clouds in the sky. Yes, it also places us on par with "god," but to do so, it first empties the idea of god of any transcendent meaning. It makes the whole more important than the parts, and drowns individualism in a sea of "everything-ism." Who you are and what you want take a backseat to the collective consciousness of the cosmos.

2. Monism leads to passivism and fatalism.

It makes no sense to struggle against evil and suffering. These things are simply what is. And what is is what is, and we're stuck with it. Consistent monists resign themselves to suffering; suffering belongs to existence as matter and energy belong to existence. It is a constituent element. Don't fight it. Accept it. It will be here forever.

3. Monism offers no coming hope or redemption.

Christians sit on the edge of their seat, waiting the day when God will overcome evil and the cosmos will be released from its curse and we shall step into the glorious liberty of the children of God (Romans 8:19-22). Monism morphs joy and pain into one thing and judges it as neither good nor bad. It sees no problem to solve except the problem of perception.

4. Monism offers little rational basis for morality and ethics.

Why should I treat you better than, say, a cow? Or a rock? "If all is one," as Manson asked, "what is bad?" I know that most monists head toward the brighter end of the spectrum, especially Oprah, but why? Why do good? Why bother? Some might say, because the good they send into the world comes back to them in a "karmic" sort of way. Is that a satisfying answer? Doesn't that make self-interest the basis of morality? How far will that take you?

A Biblical Christian Theodicy

For we know that the whole creation groans and labors with birth pangs together until now. (Romans 8:22)

We are emotional beings, so we feel pain in ourselves and others. I felt pain when my friends' baby died, and when I saw suffering Africans in a jungle hospital. Other people suffered, yet I felt pain.

I'm glad I have that ability even though sometimes it can be overwhelming. It weaves our hearts together.

Without emotions, I don't think there would be a problem of pain. We'd be like robots. We would interpret pain simply as a warning against potential damage. And we wouldn't worry much about the fairness of it all.

Think of this: if Christians did not put forth a "good" God, then we wouldn't have to justify him in light of evil and pain. Not all religions develop a theodicy; only those that teach God is good. If you knock the "God is good" corner off the so-called Inconsistent Triad, you no longer have a problem.

So would you rather have us say that God is bad? Or has ice in his veins? If you dethrone the Christian God on the basis of the problem of pain, then what are your alternatives? Do they offer comfort in your pain? Do they alleviate your pain? Do they make better sense of your pain?

I'd rather be optimistic enough to believe in an all-good, all-powerful God and struggle with the problem of evil than to kick a corner off the triangle. I'll stay more upbeat that way.

The underlying premise of the Inconsistent Triad is that a good God owes us a pain-free existence. This makes me ask why. Why does the fact that something hurts obligate God to make it stop hurting? Why? By what logic does God owe us either painlessness or pleasure? Must he create a world in which every source of pain dissolves before it does its damage? Knives that cut bread but not fingers? Fire that cooks meat, but not flesh?

C.S. Lewis nailed it when he suggested most of us don't want a Father in heaven, we want a Grandfather in heaven, "a senile benevolence... whose plan for the universe was simply that it might be truly said at the end of each day, 'a good time was had by all'."

He then points out that true love transcends our puny notions of "niceness."[13]

Lewis is right. The angels who fly around God's throne do not cry out, "Nice! Nice! Nice!" They cry out "Holy! Holy! Holy!" God is not nice; he is a consuming fire.[14] He is holy. And he is love. What does that mean? Lewis answers,

> You asked for a loving God: you have one. The great spirit you so lightly invoked... is present: not a senile benevolence that drowsily wishes you to be happy in your own way... but the consuming fire Himself, the Love that made the worlds...[15]

Sometimes true love permits pain for a greater good. Any parent who has mourned the look of betrayal from their freshly vaccinated infant understands. The therapist who made me move my shoulder after surgery understands too.

What if we couldn't feel pain? What if God did the very thing we beg him to do—"God, make it stop hurting..."—then what? Doesn't pain alert us to danger? to evil? to wounds?

Pain motivates healing action.

Without pain, you wouldn't yank your hand out of a fire, or smuggle your children out of an abusive home. There's a sense in which we should thank God for the ability to feel pain. That does not mean we should seek it, or enjoy it, or like it. It means we should listen to its message and act accordingly.

But what about senseless pain, like the Holocaust? Or intertribal genocide? Or terrorism? These fall under the category of evil, and we'll take them up in the next chapter. But for now, let me lay out the consistent view of suffering that emerges from Scripture.

Why?

The Bible treats suffering as an alien invader. It was not part of God's original creation; it wasn't his original story arc. Pain entered later, when sin and evil entered. No death, no sorrow, no suffering, and no pain existed in God's good creation. The biblical authors never blame God for the problem of pain. God didn't create evil or the suffering it birthed.

We brought that on ourselves, collectively speaking.

So, the authors of Scripture add that, when evil galloped into the world, suffering and death rode in on its back. St. Paul explains, "by one man sin entered the world"—referring to Adam—and he adds, "and death by sin" (Romans 5:12).[16]

Ultimately, Scripture reveals a God who did not stand aloof from the problem of pain; he became human without ceasing to be God, and submerged himself in the depths of pain like no other human before or since. Isaiah prophesied of Jesus on the Cross, "Many were amazed when they saw him—beaten and bloodied, so disfigured one would scarcely know he was a person" (Isaiah 52:14, NLT). Please don't think Jesus used his God-powers as a narcotic to deaden his pain. Jesus encountered the problem of pain in its fullness as a man—without resorting to his divine powers (Philippians 2:5-8).

No matter how much you hurt, you are never alone. God comes alongside you and is ready to embrace you with an empathy that knows no bounds.

There is no other belief-system that offers anything like this—not animism, not naturalism, and not monism. Because evil and suffering are alien invaders, God can remove them without altering our essential humanness. Plus, God can purge the universe of evil without purging it of humans. Whew!

Even more, God understands the problem of pain through direct experience. "Since he himself has gone through suffering and temptation, he is able to help us when we are being tempted" (Hebrews 2:18, NLT).

No other religion even comes close. No other God-became-man suffered and died as our sin-bearer. No other god satisfied the demands of cosmic justice relative to evil, while providing the final solution to the problem of pain.

If you don't like the biblical answer to the problem of pain, do you have a better one?

One last observation before I outline some talking points.

Pain is Temporary

Pain is temporary. I know, I know: my friend, Toni, just finished her twentieth surgery for chronic back pain. I'm sure her pain doesn't feel temporary. Pain never feels temporary. I'm writing this chapter ten days after my five-year old son underwent surgery. I can't describe how slowly time crawled during that procedure. Life shifted into slow motion. My wife and I would have gladly traded places with him. We couldn't stand to think of him suffering, and it seemed like forever.

Days later, however, a fog has gathered over those memories. It has grown thicker every day. I can only imagine what heaven will do to our memories of pain.

Evil and its offspring, pain, cannot be understood fully within time. One day, our limited temporal horizon will give way to an eternal perspective and we will say that God has been better to us than we ever imagined or deserved. Through the centuries, Jesus-followers have found comfort in God's astonishing promise: "For our light affliction, which is but for a moment, is working for us a far more exceeding and eternal weight of glory" (2 Corinthians 4:17).

How could a hunted, slandered, tortured, persecuted Roman prisoner like St. Paul call anybody's affliction light and momentary? I don't know what you feel like when you're hurting, but for me, pain feels heavy and forever.

So God invites us into a secret way of understanding it: *set your pain in an eternal context.*

From the standpoint of eternity, even a lifetime of pain is light and momentary. This does not minimize suffering. It does not deny that our suffering can be intense and even brutal. Scripture just puts the problem of pain into a larger context—an infinite one. Christians believe in everlasting life. We will be with God forever in heaven, with no more pain, no more sorrows, and no more tears. Pain does not have the final say. It does not win in the end. God overcomes it.

That belief carries us through.

Some people turn bitter, wondering why God created us knowing we would fall. Perhaps he saw our indescribable blessings in eternity as far outweighing the momentary difficulties of time.

But it gets better.

The most amazing part of Paul's statement is that our afflictions produce something: "a far more exceeding and eternal weight of glory." I'm not sure of all that it means, but it sounds awesome. It offers a hope that no other system promises: suffering isn't wasted. No tear is wasted. God keeps track, and it all means something.

Whatever else it means, the problem of pain means that our eyes are fixed on God, who "comforts us in all our tribulations" (2 Corinthians 1:4). What if pain is the natural outcome of not yet being with God? What if it is a necessary corollary of living outside of heaven? Perhaps pain motivates us to emotionally disinvest in time—at least a little bit—that we might invest more in eternity. No, it doesn't make life hurt any less. It just makes the pain a little more tolerable. That's a good thing.

------ # & ! $ # + % ----

Talking Points

1. No one gets to complain about the problem of pain who doesn't work to solve it.

Ask your friend, "What have you done in the last month to help solve the problem of pain?" Reducing the world's suffering has eternal significance. The causes of world missions, digging wells, teaching agriculture, building jungle hospitals, running rescue missions, serving as a Salvation Army bell-ringer, and providing ministry to the poor and oppressed are near to God's heart. Jesus takes it personally when we feed or shelter "the least of these" (Matthew 25:35-45).

If you want to put your treasure where your heart is, scan this QR code and donate to dozens of worthy causes from Sudan to Cambodia through a highly respected organization called *Samaritan's Purse.*

2. The world hurts. It is unjust and unfair, but only because we willfully rejected God as our rightful ruler and king.

We live in a fallen world and bad things happen to all (1 Corinthians 10:13; James 1:2; Matthew 5:45). We'll think through that factoid and return to the Inconsistent Triad in the next chapter.

3. God can bring good out of bad.

No other system offers this kind of hope for those who suffer (Gen. 50:20). Joseph suffered tragic losses, but God used him to save countless lives from starvation and to lead innumerable Egyptians to the worship of the true God. If Joseph's suffering resulted in multitudes being fed on earth and going to heaven after earth, was it worth it? You decide. Joseph never understood his pain until the end of his story. I have a feeling we won't either.

Though God can and does bring good out of bad, it's usually not a good thing to say when your friend is actually going through suffering. It's better to draw near, offer a listening ear, pray, and shut up.

4. Stretch your friends with this question:

Christianity offers a God who felt the fullest measure of human suffering, a Savior who comforts us in our suffering, a global mission to alleviate suffering, final justice for those who cause suffering, and a coming world that abolishes suffering... What does your system offer?

5. Offer to pray for your friend's pain.

Then pray out loud, right on the spot. This isn't about being right. It's about touching lives with the love of Jesus and serving others in his name. If your friend doesn't want your prayer, don't be indignant. Ask if it's okay to pray for something else, like genocide or famine or persecution around the world. Make sure your prayer is loving and brave.

------ # & ! $ # + % ----

CLICK IT: www.FourLetterWords.org/ouch

SCAN IT:

powered by BWSCAN.com

CHAPTER 6

Evil is just a point of view.[1]
--ANNE RICE

------ # & ! $ # + % ----

Touchy Ideas

1. God is not the source of evil.
2. Evil exists.
3. Some actions are right and some actions are wrong.
4. Evil originated with Satan, and entered the human race through mankind's free choice.
5. Though God can and will stop evil, he hasn't done it yet, and this doesn't contradict his goodness and power.

Touchy Scriptures

1. Let no one say when he is tempted, "I am being tempted by God"; for God cannot be tempted by evil, and He Himself does not tempt anyone. (James 1:13, NASB)
2. I form the light, and create darkness: I make peace, and create evil: I the LORD do all these things. (Isaiah 45:7, KJV)
3. LORD, how long shall I cry, And You will not hear? Even cry out to You, "Violence!" And You will not save. (Habakkuk 1:2)
4. You are of purer eyes than to behold evil, And cannot look on wickedness. Why do You look on those who deal treacherously, And hold Your tongue when the wicked devours a person more

righteous than he? (Habakkuk 1:13)

------ # & ! $ # + % ----

SOMETIMES YOU GET THE IMPRESSION that evil is in the eye of the beholder...

The prisoner fell to his knees as rough hands knocked him down and stripped him bare. Convinced of their God-given mission, authorities read aloud the charges against him. They announced the death sentence, and the mob roared its approval. Such evil cannot be tolerated in a righteous society—it must be stamped out.

The prisoner stretched out his hands and prayed. He begged God to forgive his executioners.

The king's soldiers tied the prisoner's hands behind his back. They wound an iron chain around his neck, and fastened him to the waiting stake. Church leaders nodded in approval as attendants stacked straw and wood around Jan Hus up to his neck. Only his head remained exposed.

On July 6, 1415, before torching the pile, the Imperial Marshal offered the Czech hero, a defrocked priest, a final chance to repent of his false teachings. "Repent, and save your life," the marshal offered.

Jan Hus refused, declaring, "In the truth of the Gospel—which I have written, taught, and preached—I will die today with gladness."

The crowd watched in fascinated horror as flames split the evildoer's skin and roasted his writhing body. The smell of burnt hair and charred flesh stung their nostrils. Ecclesiastical leaders breathed a sigh of relief. Gladness filled their hearts. Goodness prevailed that day. Evil suffered a setback. Heaven smiled.[2,3]

Or did it?

Did heaven smile when the Spanish Inquisition "preserved doctrinal purity" while torturing over 40,000 and killing over one thousand? The Inquisitors meant to rid the world of evil. But so did the heretics they killed. Just who did evil here?

Surely upgrading the human gene pool is a noble ambition, right? Did heaven smile over a dictator's plan to exterminate the mentally ill, Jews, and homosexuals to achieve that end? Was Adolf Hitler eradicating evil or perpetrating it?

What about the hijackers who downed the World Trade Centers? My missionary friends in another country told me their neighbors cheered when they heard the news. While some revered the hijackers as martyrs for a righteous cause, others cursed them as diabolical villains. Who was right?

In each case, one group's atrocity was another group's moral victory. Who defines good and evil? Who decides if an act is moral or immoral? Did literary vampire-queen, Anne Rice, get it right when she declared, "Evil is just a point of view"?

What about the Inconsistent Triad? How can a good God ignore the world's evil?

Our Schizoid Culture

Sometimes, I feel caught in a doubly schizoid culture. Split number one: we're sharply split over *moral values:* I have some friends who tag gay marriage as evil and others who tag opposition to gay marriage as evil. Some say abortion is evil; others say opposition to it is evil. Our culture is divided over moral issues ranging from global warming to eating meat, with passionate advocates and detractors on both sides. We are morally polarized. That's the first part of our schizoid culture.

But it gets worse.

Because split number two is this: we are also split over *the existence of moral values.* Many of my same friends, who get so ticked off at opponents to their moral causes, also deny the existence of moral absolutes. "It's wrong to judge people," they say. "There is no objective basis that helps us determine right and wrong. Don't cast stones."

But if you're against casting stones, isn't it inconsistent to cast stones at those who cast stones?

In the classic book, *Mere Christianity,* C. S. Lewis described his journey from atheism to Christianity. He wrote, "[As an atheist] my argument against God was that the universe seemed so cruel and unjust. But how had I got this idea of just and unjust? A man does not call a line crooked unless he has some idea of a straight line."[4] The idea of morality, he argued, can only come from God.

Once we divorce morality from God—or some other Ultimate Authority—all we can do is shout at each other. If you played pick-up sports as a kid, you understand what I mean. You kick the ball past an invisible line, and your friend calls you out of bounds. But, since you and your friend never agreed where the invisible line was to begin with, you get into a shouting match. *"No way! The line is by the trash cans, not the shrubs!"* Witness: the ongoing debates over abortion, embryonic stem cell research, and gay marriage, with both sides shouting at each other because they never agreed where the lines were drawn to begin with.

But the instant you call any play out of bounds—as soon as you say that anybody is wrong for any action whatsoever—you admit to some kind of line, some kind of absolute. Once you do that, you're on the slippery slope to believing in God, the Ultimate Linesman. And who wants God breathing down their necks?

It's much more convenient to adopt an "anything goes" approach to morality. *"It's not my place to judge."*

Maintaining this approach, however, is tougher than it sounds. Because as soon as some kleptomaniac heists your laptop from the coffee shop, you're going to cry "Foul!" And that will land you right back in the moral absolutist camp.

It's like shouting, "There are no lines!" and "You crossed a line!" in the same breath.

We're not just polarized over moral issues, we're polarized over whether there are moral issues in the first place. See what I mean by a doubly schizoid culture?

Biblical scholar, Norman Geisler, wrote, "The atheist must make his painful choice: Either he loses the basis for his argument against God from evil [by saying there is no evil], or he must admit there is an objective moral law which leads to a Moral Law Giver."[5] TRANSLATION: if you're going to argue that "evil is just a point of view," don't come crying to the authorities when a bully steals your lunch money.

So, you have two options: you can either (a) deny, or (b) accept, the existence of objective moral standards.

There's also a third, very popular, option: (c) you can switch back and forth at your convenience. You can maintain objective moral standards when they suit your day's agenda, and deny objective moral standards when they cramp your style. This option denies the laws of consistency and non-contradiction, but who's keeping score?

Because if you admit any lines whatsoever, you have to ask who drew them.

As a Christian, I believe God drew the lines. I believe he pre-programmed the most important ones into human nature, so that most cultures consider murder, abuse, rape, and cruelty wrong. God's laws, the Bible says, are written on our hearts (Romans 2:15). That makes us accountable to him, and without excuse (Romans 1:20).

It also makes us courageous under fire, which is why Jan Hus refused to compromise his belief in the gospel, with horrific ramifications.

Once you fire God from his job as Moral Linesman, you're going to have a hard time replacing him. Everyone wants to draw his or her own lines. That's what's happening in Western civilization today. Our moral playing field looks like it was drawn by a class of blindfolded six-year-olds, hopped up on sugar cubes. When postmodernism undermined intellectual truth, it undermined moral boundaries too. When we shoved biblical values out the back door, good and evil sauntered through the front door and got married.

So now who draws the lines? Let me offer a guided tour two popular options, and then bring it home to God's Inconsistent Triad.

Who Draws Today's Moral Lines?

You can divide theories of evil into two squabbling camps: moral relativists and moral absolutists.

Moral Relativism

Moral relativists believe that each society decides good and evil for itself. Right and wrong are situation-specific shape-shifters. Morality cannot be etched in stone; it varies over time, and shifts to suit the culture. Right and wrong are right and wrong because we say so – "we" meaning the dominant culture of the times.

Moral relativism and postmodernism play nicely together. Like postmodern truth, postmodern morals are fluid. Here are some key features of moral relativism:

Unwillingness to cast stones. Relativists love Jesus' statement: "He who is without sin among you, let him throw a stone at her first." (John 8:7). Because of this, relativists often come across as more forgiving than most Christians. That's unfortunate for a movement launched by the Prince of Forgiveness.

Dislike of absolutists. When Christians state their positions in absolute terms, relativists look at us like we're the Amish. Why don't you just hop in your buggy and trot along? Tell university students that God made sex for married couples and they'll ask what planet you came from. If truth is relative, there's only room for one commandment: You shall not believe in absolutes... or else I'll wash your mouth out with soap.

Moral tolerance. Today's moral relativists adopt a "live and let live" policy toward their neighbors. In some ways, this is a huge improvement over our often judgmental, hyper-critical religious ancestors. But, I have to wonder how far this tolerance should go.

Would you tolerate drug dealers next door? A prostitution ring? You could never say where you'd draw the lines, because you've already decided there are no lines.

Moral Subjectivism. Instead of a broad moral code for everybody, radical relativism makes room for individualized moral codes that differ from person to person. I have my own moral code and you have yours. This position, called subjectivism, is nothing new. Over twelve centuries before Jesus, the Bible warned, "In those days there was no king in Israel; everyone did what was right in his own eyes" (Judges 17:6). I don't want to live next to a neighbor with radically subjective morality, especially if he stockpiles weapons or thinks it's okay to mess with kids.

Relativism's Meteoric Rise

It took moral relativism only two or three generations to win over Western Civilization. Here are some findings from the Barna Research Group:[6]

- "People were asked if they believe that there are moral absolutes that are unchanging or that moral truth is relative to the circumstances. By a 3-to-1 margin (64% vs. 22%) adults said that truth is always relative to the person and their situation.
- "Among teenagers, 83% said moral truth depends on the circumstances, and only 6% said moral truth is absolute.
- "Among adults, only 32% of those who were born again said they believe in moral absolutes.
- "Among teenagers, just 9% of born again teens believe in moral absolutes."

This shift to relativism isn't just evolution, it's revolution, and we're only beginning to feel its impact. Our grandparents remember a simpler day, when good guys were easy to tell from bad guys. When Superman fought for "truth, justice, and the American way." They remember the days of moral absolutism.

Moral Absolutism

Moral absolutism is the belief that there are absolute standards against which moral questions can be judged. "[C]ertain actions are right or wrong, no matter the context of the act."[7] According to moral absolutists, right and wrong flow out of an objective lawgiver, like nature or God.

The American founders grounded their War for Independence in moral absolutism. They argued, "All men are created equal, and are endowed by their Creator with certain inalienable rights..." For them, "life, liberty, and the pursuit of happiness" were supreme values, not because they felt good in the current climate (relativism), but because a Higher Power granted these rights to mankind (absolutism).

Some identified that Higher Power as the God of the Bible. Others saw him as a nameless Creator. In either case, they described human freedom as flowing from a source above the laws of mankind. Since human rulers did not grant these rights, human rulers couldn't take them away. To them, the ABCs of morality were God-given absolutes that flew above a turbulent sea of moral currents and cultural trends.

Some absolutists worry that the recent shift toward relativism signals the end of civilization. C.S. Lewis wrote,

> Out of this apparently innocent idea [relativism] comes the disease that will certainly end our species (and, in my view, damn our souls) if it is not crushed; the fatal superstition that men can create values, that a community can choose

its 'ideology' as men choose their clothes.[8]

Apparently Lewis was not a fan of relativism. He makes an important point: pollute morality at its source, and you poison the whole stream. A morality based on the latest fad makes the culture flaky, and ends up hurting people. What's to stop me—or a government—from threatening your life, trampling your liberty, or messing with your pursuit of happiness? Why shouldn't a dictator declare other values to be supreme, like Conformity and the State? Picture millions of children, wearing uniforms, marching in perfect step to a dictator's tune. Picture the Borg on *Star Trek*.

Without absolutism, might makes right. The toughest bully runs the schoolyard.

Philosopher Immanuel Kant expressed moral absolutism when he wrote, "two things fill the soul with ever new and increasing wonder and reverence the oftener and more fervently reflection ponders on it: the starry heavens above and the moral law within."[9] The Bible says God's moral law has been written on our hearts.

That means the only way to escape God's laws is to numb yourself to your own heart. That is the unhappy result of relativism. But we're still seeing our culture race to the relativist camp. Why?

Because absolutism makes people squirm. It renders us *accountable.*

Most of us are allergic to accountability.

The question is simple: is there even one moral law that should never be violated?

If you say yes, you are accountable to that law.

If you say no, you have no rational basis for morality and no way to ever evaluate right and wrong.

On a late night, fast-food run with my friend, Kevin, we stopped at a deserted intersection in a frigid Chicago winter and contemplated moral absolutes. It was after midnight. There were only two cars on the street. I was westbound on Grand Avenue. A second car was eastbound. We both sat at the same red light, in the dead of night, with no cross traffic, no other vehicles, and no police cars in sight. We could have blown the red light with no fear of tickets or collisions. But there we sat, waiting for green. As we sat there, we devoured Chicago hot dogs and grease-soaked French fries from the bags on our laps.

I turned to Kevin and said, "The fact that we've both stopped at this light gives me hope." At least two drivers that night yielded to objective standards outside themselves.

You're probably figuring that I'm going to slam relativism and exalt absolutism, and you'll be wrong. It's not that easy.

Moral absolutism, at its best, brings harmony and order to society. It allows no one to be above the law. It buttresses our integrity, and allows us to live peacefully with our neighbors. At its worst, it makes us harsh judges who sacrifice the spirit for the letter of the law. It can make us bow to tyrants.

Moral relativism, at its best, breaks through legalistic shackles, and allows us freedom to be ourselves. It nurtures a "live and let live" spirit, and allows us to coexist with our unconventional neighbors. At its worst, relativism makes us either spineless anarchists or arrogant little lords, usurping God's place, and standing in judgment over his laws.

Should Christians switch back and forth between relativism and absolutism? Let's ask Jesus.

Jesus on Evil

1. Jesus upheld the Old Testament laws.

He said, "Do not think that I came to destroy the Law or the Prophets. I did not come to destroy but to fulfill" (Matthew 5:17). In his next breath, he promised that not even the smallest detail of God's law would be overlooked. Jesus respected the Law of Moses—which includes the Ten Commandments—as an absolute. By Jesus' day, those laws were 1,400 years old. Moral fads came and went, but God's laws remained the same.

2. Jesus routinely shocked his listeners with God's absolute standards.

He set the moral bar impossibly high:

- Therefore you shall be perfect, just as your Father in heaven is perfect (Matthew 5:48).
- For I say to you, that unless your righteousness exceeds the righteousness of the scribes and Pharisees [the ultra-religious], you will by no means enter the kingdom of heaven (Matthew 5:20).

By those standards, nobody qualified for heaven. Jesus drew a moral dividing line. He upheld absolute standards.

3. Jesus seemed to contradict some Old Testament laws... but he actually upheld them.

Jesus apparently contrasted his teaching with the law of Moses. Here are two examples:

- You have heard that the law of Moses says, 'Do not murder. If you commit murder, you are subject to judgment.' But I say, if you are angry with someone, you are subject to judgment... (Matthew 5:21,22, NLT).

- You have heard that the law of Moses says, 'If an eye is in-
  jured, injure the eye of the person who did it. If a tooth gets
  knocked out, knock out the tooth of the person who did it.'
  But I say, don't resist an evil person! If you are slapped on the
  right cheek, turn the other, too (Matthew 5:38, 39, NLT).

Does Jesus really have a problem with the law of Moses—the
absolutes that guided the Jews for fourteen centuries? If he adapted
God's moral law for a new era, he might be a flaming relativist,
right?

Some scholars think so. But if you look carefully at these verses,
you'll see that Jesus isn't contradicting the Old Testament laws; he's
doing something else.

He's insisting that the super-holy religious frauds of his day
keep God's laws inwardly and not just outwardly. One Bible scholar
explains it like this:

> Jesus maintains that obedience or disobedience to the law
> begins inwardly, in the human heart. It was not sufficient
> to conform one's outward actions and words to what the
> law required; the thought-life must be conformed to it
> first of all.[10]

Jesus swam in a sea of people who obeyed God's law in their
actions but violated it in their *attitudes*. The law of Moses, which
these guys claimed to uphold so flawlessly, required obedience from
the heart. Jesus didn't make this up. Moses, the original lawgiver,
did:

> And the LORD your God will circumcise your heart and
> the heart of your descendants, to love the LORD your
> God with all your heart and with all your soul, that you
> may live (Deuteronomy 30:6).

Jesus wasn't adapting God's laws to a new era; he was fulfilling them to a depth the Jews forgot about. You might argue, "Hey, Wise Guy, if Jesus didn't adapt God's laws, then when's your next goat sacrifice? How come you put bacon and cheese on your burger? Isn't that relativizing God's laws?"

Not if certain sections of God's laws had built-in obsolescence, like the toys I buy my kids at the megastore. The ancient sacrifices and dietary laws were early symbols of Jesus. The Bible calls them a "shadow" of Christ (Colossians 2:17). They were like flashing neon signs pointing to the coming Savior. Once he came, the Bible's ceremonial and ritual laws had finished their job, so they rode off into the sunset. That's why God told Peter, a kosher Jew, to eat non-kosher meat (Acts 10:1-16), why Paul said to "let no one judge" us in regard to Sabbaths and religious festivals (Colossians 2:16), and why the Bible said those old ceremonies would "vanish away" (Hebrews 8:13). That was always the plan since the day those laws were written.

For Jesus, ceremonial laws came and went, but God's moral laws never changed. That's because they flow out of God's heart. God's laws are God's laws because God's nature is God's nature. For God to change his laws, he'd have to change his nature. Disney will build an admission-free theme park on the surface of the sun before that happens.

The Real Inconsistent Triad

It's time to return to the Inconsistent Triad, the idea that three ideas can't all be true: 1) The existence of evil. 2) An all-good God. 3) An all-powerful God.

I'd like to propose a different Inconsistent Triad, one that I think makes more sense. Here's the Real Inconsistent Triad; see if you can wrap these three concepts into a package that passes the logical sniff test:

1. Personal Beings. People like us, with individuality, self-consciousness, and a will to survive and thrive. We exist, and we are not mindless robots.

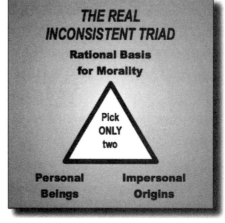

2. Impersonal Origins. We humanoids, with all our personality and color, are cosmic accidents of matter and energy. We have more personality than whatever made us. Everything we do and think, according to some, is the product of DNA and maybe last night's pizza.

3. A Rational Basis for Morality. Other than self-interest, why should I be nice to you? Why should I respect my neighbor, if she's nothing more than a complex light bulb (nothing against my actual neighbor who is an excellent person)?

There's no way to package these three concepts without kissing at least a little common sense good-bye. Yet if you poll 50 people on the street, 47 of them will be munching this self-contradicting apple in blissful unawareness.

We have created a society with craziness at its core. We have created a culture that either robs people of personhood or empties morality of meaning. We are gagging on the revolutionary pill we swallowed in the 1960's, just as predicted by philosopher/theologian Francis Schaeffer:

> We are watching our culture put into effect the fact that
> when you tell men long enough that they are machines,

it soon begins to show in their actions. You see it in our whole culture—in the theatre of cruelty, in the violence in the streets, in the death of man in art and life.[11]

Is human life precious? Then consuming it is evil. I'm just arguing that some actions are wrong, and some actions aren't. You might wonder how this lets God off the hook. Isn't he still responsible for the world's bad stuff?

Theodicy One Last Time

Jesus and the rest of Scripture writers said no. Jesus found the source of evil not in God, but in the devil (John 8:44). I know this raises all kinds of questions about worldview and supernaturalism. But humor me long enough to make my point.

My point is that God is not the author of evil, according to the biblical worldview. God can be both all-powerful and all-good while at the same time letting evil afflict the world. In other words, the Inconsistent Triad isn't inconsistent.

Let's think together how this can be.

1. Absolutes flow from God.

Right and wrong are right and wrong because of the nature of God. Goodness flows from him and is defined by him. That means good and evil are more than just a point of view.

The Ten Commandments are the Ten Commandments because they reflect God's heart. They reflect his love and concern for the human race. They are not arbitrary laws for another time and place. They are everlasting laws for all people because they flow from the heart of a God who wants to protect us humans from destroying ourselves and others.

2. Humans are fallen, in an abnormal state.

As we exist now, we are not as God made us. "The Fall" is the event in history when the human race chose against God. We did this at the dawn of civilization through our earthly father Adam. Satan seduced Eve, who seduced Adam, who thumbed his nose at God.

We swan-dived into sin, eyes wide open. The Fall opened a door to evil. It invited death and cruelty in the world. It distorted our nature and triggered our self-destruct sequence. We asked for it.

But God is greater than it. Evil is temporary. It's a blip on God's eternal radar. One day, God will exterminate it. To us, evil seems huge. That's because we have a limited perspective—we see from the standpoint of time. From an eternal standpoint, however, evil is a one-hit-wonder. It is an alien God tolerates for reasons we can't know, but an alien that will one day be permanently banished from his presence.

It will be banished from our very beings, too. This sets Christianity in a class by itself. Since evil is an intruder, and not part of our original nature, God can yank the evil out of us without altering our essential humanness. When God rolls out his cosmic end-game, and exterminates the evil infesting you, you will, for the first time in your existence, be normal.

Your mom just shouted *Hallelujah*.

3. Jesus is the final solution for cosmic evil.

Jesus died to crush evil's head—and that includes removing the venom it injected into you.

If you take away absolute morality, the death of Christ makes no sense. It was a colossal waste of an epic life, and a wildly overblown subplot on the world's stage.

But if God's standards stand sure, the Cross makes more sense than any other redemptive scheme ever imagined. It is the only way God can satisfy his infinite justice and his boundless love at the same time. He satisfies his justice by punishing sin in a way that removes it. He satisfies his love by forgiving us. "Behold the Lamb of God who *takes away* the sin of the world" (John 1:29).

Think about this: without the Cross, the universe floats along without any final answer to evil. Without the Cross, evil wins; it is everlasting. Without the Cross, the scales of justice remain imbalanced forever. When your friends challenge God on the basis of evil, challenge them back. Ask them what religion offers a better solution for the problem of evil.

You can make your skeptical friends squirm even more with another question.

If evil is "just a point of view," then how can you criticize God for allowing it? "I don't believe in evil" and "I don't believe in God because he allows/creates evil" can't go together.

The Christian worldview says that Christ will stamp out evil and sin and death. It's a two-step dance: Evil's head was crushed at the Cross, and the tail will be finished at the Last Judgment.

4. Christians have a rational ground for fighting evil and social injustice.

In fact, we have the only rational ground. We can fight evil without fighting God. *Monists* can't, because good and evil and god are all one; to fight evil is to fight god. *Dualists* can't, because good and evil are equal; to fight evil is to fight a losing battle. *Naturalists* can't, because there is no evil to fight—just machines doing what they're programmed to do. If natural selection improves the gene pool, shouldn't we step away from our war against evil? Shouldn't we let nature pick off the weakest of our species? Wouldn't we all be better off if we just let cosmic cruelty play itself out?

But *Christians* can fight evil without self-contradiction. When Jesus visited the tomb of his friend, Lazarus, he got emotional. He was sad, and he was mad. Jesus couldn't accept the cosmic status quo. He knew that things are not the way they're supposed to be. Death is an abnormal cruelty; an intruder God did not create, and Jesus hated it.

So he gave a mini-preview of a major coming attraction: Jesus raised Lazarus from the dead and promised he was just getting warmed up.

When we fight death and evil, we're following his steps. We Christians should be on the front lines fighting human cruelty and evil—not because we're in love with morality, but because we're in love with God and the innumerable people he loves.

More Than a Point of View

I started this chapter with a quote from Anne Rice about evil being "a point of view." Anne Rice is best known for vampire-themed Gothic novels. She has sold over 100 million books, and has seen them translated into movies, stage plays, television shows and songs. She has written horror, historical fiction, and pornography.

The Queen of Vampires wrote out of her own pain. Raised Catholic, Rice turned away from God after the death of her six-year-old daughter from leukemia. I have two little kids, and can't imagine that agony. My heart goes out to her.

Later, the death of her sixty-year-old husband from brain cancer only added to her grief. Rice poured her despair into vampire stories.

The problem of evil obliterated her faith. For Rice, mankind's quest for meaning was doomed to fail.

Then, something big happened.

Anne Rice, famous atheist, became Anne Rice, committed Christian. In coming to Christ, she found her own answer to the problem of evil. She said,

> On the afternoon in 1998 when faith returned, I experienced a sense of the limitless power and majesty of God that left me convinced that He knew all the answers to the theological and sociological questions that had tormented me for years. I saw, in one enduring moment, that the God who could make the Double Helix and the snow flake, the God who could make the Black holes in space, and the lilies of the field, could do absolutely

anything and must know everything—even why good people suffer, [and] why genocide and war plague our planet...[12]

Rice didn't find her answer to the problem of evil in philosophical arguments. She found it in the majesty of God. In the intricacy of a snowflake and the enormity of black holes.

I am not claiming to prove Christianity. I am claiming it's plausible, and I'm asking doubters to come up with something more plausible. And something as beautiful.

Jesus satisfies me. Logically. Emotionally. Spiritually.

I've never found a better belief system;

I've never found a better friend.

In this evil world, life hurts. But my good God, through Jesus, pulled the stinger out.

------ # & ! $ # + % ----

Talking Points

1. When your friends criticize God for allowing evil, ask them to define evil.

Don't get defensive. When they say, "I can't believe a loving God would allow all the evil in the world," just ask, "How do you define evil?" Then ask them who gets to define evil, us or God? Why should God be accountable to our definitions of evil? Doesn't that flip over the truth? Yes, God allows evil in the world, but what if it serves purposes better than we can imagine?

2. Only people who believe in God have a rational reason to fight evil.

If you are a naturalist, who believes in evolution, there is no evil to fight. So fighting an oppressive government is like fighting a pack of sharks, and battling world hunger is battling natural selection—we're all just doing what we're genetically programmed to do.

If you're into Wicca or other pagan religions, evil is just a point of view. In your view, we should "live and let live" and it's wrong to fight other people's point of view.

If you are a monist, evil is an illusion. Good, evil, god, mankind, and all things are part of the cosmic oneness. To fight evil is to fight yourself. And god.

If you are a dualist who believes in a yin-yang balance of opposites, to you, good and evil are equals, like mirror-image twins. Evil can never be overcome, because it's a natural part of existence. All you can do is shift the evil from one place to another, like squeezing one end of a balloon.

3. If we argue for moral absolutes, then our lives should be our best argument.

What do our seeking friends think when we talk about God's standards and then live selfish lives, get stoned, cheat on our wives, and trash the planet? We believe God's laws represent the highest possible expression of love. Jesus said so (Mark 12:30,31 and Romans 13:9). To love our neighbors, we have to obey God's laws—without making the Bible a buffet of options we can take or leave. When we do that, our critics lose ammunition. Love is the only defense of Christianity no one can debate.

4. Our belief in absolutes is not a hall-pass to be a jerk.

We can play within God's moral lines and not be idiots toward those who have crossed them. Christians have to stop being crabby and judgmental. That's not the spirit of Jesus. We believe what we believe, and are patient and charitable with our friends who disagree.

We are supremely tolerant. We are also heartbroken, because we see how our friends damage their own hearts when they fight God. Christians should quit being ticked off by other people's sins; the Lord knows we have enough of our own. May God give us Paul's perspective: "By the grace of God I am what I am" (1 Corinthians 15:10).

------ # & ! $ # + % ----

CLICK IT: www.FourLetterWords.org/evil

SCAN IT:

powered by BWSCAN.com

Most people are bothered by those passages of Scripture they do not understand, but the passages that bother me are those I do understand.[1]
ATTRIBUTED TO MARK TWAIN

------ # & ! $ # + % ----

Touchy Ideas

1. The Bible is the inspired Word of God.
2. The Bible is God's only and final Word, in its own class, above all other religious literature.
3. The theology and ethics of the Bible transcend time and culture and are as applicable today as when originally written.
4. No other book has improved society or benefited mankind as much as the Bible.

Touchy Scriptures

1. So Moses came and called for the elders of the people, and laid before them all these words which the LORD commanded him. (Exodus 19:7)
2. I have not departed from the commandment of His lips; I have treasured the words of His mouth More than my necessary food. (Job 23:12)
3. The Holy Spirit spoke rightly through Isaiah the prophet to our fathers. (Acts 28:25)
4. All Scripture is given by inspiration of God, and is profitable for doctrine, for reproof, for correction, for instruction in

righteousness, that the man of God may be complete, thoroughly equipped for every good work. (2 Timothy 3:16,17)

5. For prophecy never came by the will of man, but holy men of God spoke as they were moved by the Holy Spirit. (2 Peter 1:21)

6. Behold, I am coming quickly! Blessed is he who keeps the words of the prophecy of this book. (Revelation 22:7)

------ # & ! $ # + % ----

I'LL NEVER FORGET THE FIRST TIME I opened *Evidence That Demands a Verdict*. First published in 1972, the book rocketed to best-seller status. Josh McDowell blew my high-school mind with his flawless logic and undeniable evidence for Christianity. He spoke my language. His book assembled massive amounts of data to support the Bible as God's Word and Jesus as God's Son. When I read his book, I felt excited. It was like an encyclopedia of unbeatable arguments for Christianity.

Surely my skeptical friends would be convinced: Scripture was true! Jesus is real! God rules! No doubt at all. That's how I felt, at least.

To my young mind, McDowell proved beyond doubt that no other religious book compares with the Bible in terms of the number and quality of ancient copies. He laid out proof of Christ's resurrection that would stand in any court. He contrasted the Bible's historical accuracy with the inaccuracies of other religious works. McDowell made the case. He put forth evidence that demanded a verdict.

I thought any rational reader would be convinced.

I was wrong.

For most people, the jury is still out on the Bible. I don't know if it's postmodern cynicism toward truth, or our inborn allergy to accountability. Maybe it's a sincere disagreement with the facts, but the evidence that looks so conclusive to me is blatantly inconclusive for a whole lot of my friends.

But for me, there is something about the Bible that sets it in a class by itself. Unfortunately, I can't prove it like a scientist can prove that a virus causes the flu. It's hard to subject the Bible's claims to empirical or rational verification.

So I won't try. You can find hundreds of excellent websites and books that make the case for the Bible from logic, evidence, and history (you can find links on the Four Letter Words website). I'm all for that, and I'm convinced. But in this chapter, I'd like to take a different approach.

I'd like to look at the Bible's beauty and love.

Whose God is Love?

In the history of world religion, it is Christianity alone—drawing from its roots in Judaism—that demolished preconceptions by offering a God of boundless love. If you erase the Bible from history, good luck finding an all-loving deity.

Here are nine major religious perspectives and their core concept of god:

Buddhism

Buddhists do not proclaim a god of love, because Buddhists do not proclaim any god at all. According to BuddhaNet, a major online resource,

> There is no almighty God in Buddhism. There is no one to hand out rewards or punishments on a supposedly [sic]

Judgement [sic] Day. Buddhism is strictly not a religion in the context of being a faith and worship owing allegiance to a supernatural being.[2]

Buddhists, like Hindus and others, believe in karma, a soulless force that makes sure the bad guys get what's coming to them—either in this life or the next life, or the next life after that. No doubt, Buddhists can be kind and loving people. But, if you need a God of Love, look elsewhere.

Islam

The one God, Allah, is bigger than, and outside of, creation. Though we can know his will, we cannot know him personally. Muslims do not normally speak of a relationship with Allah. Even when they speak of God's mercy, it is usually set in the context of justice rather than relationship. One Islamic scholar states, "God does not reveal Himself to anyone."[3] Instead, he reveals his will, and we're stuck with it. No one can question *kismet*—the unbending will of Allah. The God of Islam leads with authority, not love.

Hinduism

I struck up a conversation with a gas station attendant in Los Angeles. A calendar hung on the wall behind him with a drawing of a man in a golden suit. I asked the attendant about the picture, figuring it was a politician or celebrity. He answered, "Oh, that is god."

The calendar displayed a different god for each month. Scholars debate how to classify Hinduism.

By offering a menu of thousands of gods, it is *polytheistic*. By claiming that ultimately all things dissolve into oneness—including the gods—it is *pantheistic*. By suggesting that all gods are aspects of a single Supreme Being, it resembles *monotheism*. Hindus are comfortable in all three camps.

The main gods of Hinduism form a kind of trinity: Brahma, Vishnu and Shiva. "They are respectively the creator, preserver and destroyer of the universe."[4] Each one has a female partner-god or consort. Though some of the gods may love their people—especially Devi, the Mother-Warrior goddess—Hinduism offers no all-supreme god of boundless love.

Animism

Animists find spirits lurking behind all things, including people, animals, plants, rocks, streams, trees, and thunderstorms. When the spirits are angry, worshippers appease them through rituals, spells, and sacrifice. In the past, this has included human sacrifice. The spirits of animism do not love mankind in any special sense. Most animists resonate more with *fear* than with *love*.

Deism

There is a Supreme Being who created the universe and no longer interferes with its operations. Deists throw out any idea of miracles or supernatural influence in the world. Thomas Jefferson stitched together his own Bible by literally using scissors to cut out Scriptures he judged miraculous and therefore unworthy of Jesus. He claimed the true history and sayings of Jesus shined out from the false ones, "like diamonds on a dung heap."[5] He left the dung heap in the dung heap, and pasted up a 48-page Bible. It told the story of Jesus from his birth (minus angels and a virginal mother) to his burial (minus a resurrection).

Deism offers an emotionally icy God of High I.Q. who watches from a distance, like a father who left behind a pile of money, and then abandoned his family.

Atheism

There is no god of love because there is no god. Would it annoy you if I pointed out again that ideas have consequences?

Strip mankind of its Creator God of Love, and the most heinous crimes become not only thinkable, but actual. It is estimated that Communism—in the service of atheism—has slaughtered more humans than any other system ever devised. *Death by Government* author R. J. Rummel, estimates that Communism in the Soviet Union, China, and Cambodia, killed (or let die) over 110,000,000 people—almost three times the number of humans who died in all the world's wars during the twentieth century.[6]

Before you accuse me of breaking the needle on the "moron-meter," I'm not painting every atheist as a genocidal maniac. One of my good friends is an atheist, and he's a good-hearted, thoughtful, fun-loving guy. But how can you subtract God's love from the core of the cosmos, and expect the world's rulers to curb their lust for power? Why should they?

Wicca

Wicca is an animist religion, and like animism, believes in the spirits of trees and rocks and birds. Through spells, incantations, and rituals, Wiccans hope to persuade these spirits to play nice. They gather gods and goddesses from many other religions into a polythe-istic buffet: choose which god you need at any given time.[7] Wiccans can exhibit great love for others; I have a couple of ex-Wiccans in my church, and they are kind-hearted people. But while they were in Wicca, no one ever offered them a God of love.

Gnosticism

This ancient philosophy/religion is on the rise, thanks to movies and books like *The DaVinci Code.* It comes in many flavors and gloms onto a lot of religions: Gnostic Christianity, Gnostic Judaism, Gnostic Islam (the g is silent). It's basically a shape-shifter, except for a few core beliefs: Gnostics taught that matter was evil (your body), and spirit was good (your soul, all the invisible stuff). Since god is good, he has nothing to do with humans made of matter, like us. So he didn't create us, and doesn't relate to us. Instead, he spun off legions of mini-gods, called *emanations* or *demi-urges,* who spun off their own mini-gods, who eventually spun off mankind.

In essence, the Gnostic god distanced himself from filthy humans by creating myriads of go-betweens, like clerks in a government office, whose main job is to shield the boss from rabble like us.

Can you feel the love?

Ancient Pantheons

A *pantheon* is a roster of gods, and the ancient world offered loads of them. Egyptian, Greek, Roman, and Norse pantheons listed literally hundreds of gods.[8] None of the big ones—Ra, Zeus, Jupiter, or Odin—could ever be mistaken as a god of love. Yes, there was love and an occasional spasm of kind-heartedness from them. But it never dawned on ancient people that an

Almighty Creator God loved them and had their best interests at heart.

I attended three colleges and flipped through five majors to finally get a bachelor's degree. During my stint at the University of Illinois (Chicago), I was one of a handful of "Classics" majors. We studied Greek and Roman languages, literature, and culture. I took my first classes in ancient Greek with a Jesuit priest named Father Tracy. Good stuff.

But I don't remember ever hearing about any deity's love in any of my classes. Credit Jesus and his people for first injecting a loving God into the theological bloodstream.

God Is...

The Apostle John detonated a religious explosion when he wrote, "God is love" (1 John 4:8). He actually wrote it twice (v. 16). No other religion ever made love the heartbeat of God.

Christians *own* "God is love."

We might not have always radiated his ideal standards, but we've never budged from this mother of all religious premises. We don't simply say God *has* love, or that God *shows* love, or that God—after he's been fed enough sacrifices—is *loving*. No. We say, God *is* love. Followers of Jesus brought that message to the world. Like the original, original, Original Pancake House, there are many copies, but only one original.

That original, found in John's first Epistle, only echoes a thousand whispers of biblical teaching. John didn't invent this truth; he only summarized it from all that Scripture already said.

He supremely learned it from Jesus. Jesus taught, "Greater love has no one than this, than to lay down one's life for his friends" (John 15:13) and, "For God so loved the world that He gave His only begotten Son, that whoever believes in Him should not perish but have everlasting life" (John 3:16).

Does love prove the superiority of the Bible? Only if a loving God is important to you. Otherwise, it makes no difference.

The Main Thing

The love of God is the main theme of the whole Bible. The different authors of the Bible's sixty-six books, hold up God's love like a diamond, and make it sparkle from a million angles.

Moses highlighted this love as part of God's abiding marriage covenant with his people. If God was jealous, it was only because the people he loved went after other lovers.

David composed songs about God's love—friend to friend, and man to God. For David, God wasn't just "the Big Guy up there," he was closer than a brother, and more gentle than a shepherd.

The Prophets painted God's love as a portrait of a mother nursing her child, or a lover wooing his beloved. "The LORD has appeared

THE WRITING PROPHET
PUBLIC DOMAIN/GUTENBURG.ORG

of old to me, saying: 'Yes, I have loved you with an everlasting love; Therefore with loving-kindness I have drawn you'" (Jeremiah 31:3).

The Gospels depict God's love as a fire burning in Jesus' heart.

Sometimes it was warm and tender: when Jesus ate fish with his disciples, when he turned water to wine, and when he healed lepers and embraced society's outcasts. Other times, his love burned red hot: when he drove the crooks out of the temple with a homemade whip, when he shredded the Pharisees for loading impossible burdens on people who sought God, and when he died for our sins—the Lamb of God who took away the sin of the world.

The Epistles (most of the rest of the New Testament) analyze God's love. They tell us it flows from the heart of God in infinite measure, and that it's grounded in the death of Christ. These books humble us by comparing our puny love to God's massive love: "This is real love. It is not that we loved God, but that he loved us and sent his Son as a sacrifice to take away our sins" (1 John 4:10, NLT).

Every major part of the Bible teaches the love of God. In symbols, in ceremonies, in parables, in healings, in miracles, and in plain teaching, the love of God pulses from the Bible's beginning to its end.

Search the religious literature of the world. Dig through the annals of history. Explore religious books from any culture, anywhere in the world. You'll never find a match to the Bible's beautiful claim that God is love.

Yes, God is more than love. But that he is love, and that his love is such a big part of him, makes me feel secure. In the Bible, I read a grand narrative of a God who made me, lost me, and loved me enough to buy me back at immeasurable cost. I feel safe with this God, and safe in his universe, now and forever. God's love is a crazy big love, and I'm glad to rest in it.

Because of Love

Even so, we who follow Jesus still get in trouble for believing the Bible. How can we be so narrow to say that the Bible is God's only book? Hasn't God revealed himself in all the religions of humankind?

I know I'm only digging my hole deeper with some friends in this conversation, but I will say that if there is any truth or goodness in any other religious book or teacher, it is only a distorted memory from a race created by the Bible's God, but now wandering in darkness away from him. The Bible's teaching is original. Everything else is a copy of a copy of a copy.

I'll hold up my shields till the spitballs subside.

If a God of love has inspired any book, the only real contender is the Bible.

For the sake of argument, let's hypothesize, a) a God who is too big for finite minds to comprehend, and, b) a human race that has jumped off a moral cliff into falleness and sin.

If this is the case, we are doubly blinded in our search for God. As St. Paul told the philosophers on Mars Hill, we're groping in the dark because of both our finiteness and our falleness (Acts 17:27). We can't even begin to imagine God correctly. Fallen people can't depict God without smudging the picture. If I gave my six year old a box of crayons and told him to draw the far side of the moon, he'd do a better job of it than the world's wisest sages trying to draw a picture of God. The gap between Creator and creation is that big.

If there is going to be any true knowledge of God, it has to be because God takes the initiative to reveal himself first. That brings us back to epistemology, which brings us back to divine self-revelation, which brings us back to faith, which brings us back to the authority of the Bible.

But why should God reveal himself? Does he owe us a correct revelation of himself? Really? Says who? Why can't he stay hidden and leave us to wander the human zoo, like the Deists say he did?

He can, but he didn't.

Because of love.

God wants us to know him. To relate to him. That's why you'll hear Jesus types talk about "a personal relationship" with God.

God ripped away the veil that hid his face, and announced, "Here I am!" He wove his markers into the fabric of our universe. In the stars, the clouds, the rivers and the mountains, we see his power. He is not nature, but his mind imagined and hand made nature and its beauty. And, in nature, we can see a tiny fraction of his artistic heart and extravagant creativity.

But nature's revelation only takes us so far. We need something more.

Enter the Bible. God deposited an enduring truth into the human race. Not just a roster of commandments, though that's included. Not just a consultant's wise advice, or the epic of mankind's origin and destiny, though those are in the Bible too.

The Bible goes farther.

The Bible lays bare God's own heart for the world. His nature. His character. His attributes. His names. His works. His longings. His promises. His identity. The Bible is God's self-disclosure to any-one who's interested.

The amazing thing is that God used regular people to tell his story. He got into their lives, and they recorded their experiences. In sharp contrast to any other religious book, the Bible walks God through the tangible history of a struggling people called the Jews, and his interactions with them. The Bible puts flesh on theology. You won't find that in the *Eddas*, the *Analects*, the *Bhagavad-Gita*, the *Vedas*, the *Qur'an*, the *Upanishads* or any other sacred text. There is no book like the Bible.

Jesus-followers believe that the infinite Creator God loved us so much he revealed himself. He revealed himself in the miracle of nature and in amazing works in history. But he saved his clearest self-revelation for the Bible. It's not just a preacher-thing to call the Bible God's love note to the human race; it's a radical truth.

But it gets better, because God didn't just lob a truth-book into the world.

He lobbed Himself.

The Ultimate Word

If thoughts flow out in words, then Jesus is the fullest possible Word of God. So the New Testament nicknamed Jesus, "the Word" (John 1:1,14). And Jesus said that anyone who has seen him has seen God (John 14:9).

You might scold me for proving the Bible by quoting the Bible. I'm not. Instead, I'm building a case that the Bible is a book of love from a God of love, and is, therefore, in a class by itself.

Even Jesus thought so.

Jesus, the Living Word, put his personal seal of approval on the Bible, the written Word. Don't forget that two-thirds of the Bible was complete by Jesus' day. Growing up Jewish meant growing up Bible-smart. Picture barefoot little Jesus trotting off to synagogue holding Mary and Joseph's hands. At age twelve, he held his own in a Bible debate with the leading Rabbis of his day (Luke 2:46). He grew up with a written Word from God.

As an adult, he put his stamp of approval upon that Word. Here are some of his teachings:

- "The Scripture cannot be broken" (John 10:35).
- The Bible is indestructible until "all has been fulfilled," down to the letter (Matthew 5:18).
- The Bible is "that which was spoken to you by God" (Matthew 22:31).
- The Bible, in all its parts, unfolds truth about Jesus—about who he would be and what he would do when he came (Luke 24:27,44).

It's logically conceivable Jesus was wrong (I don't believe that, but it's conceivable). But what isn't conceivable is that Jesus was both a Great Teacher, worthy of our devotion, AND that he staked his life on a book of mistakes OR that he taught his followers to stake their eternal hopes on flawed teachings. In the mind of Jesus, everything he was and did and believed resonated perfectly with every syllable of the Scriptures.

It doesn't make sense to honor Jesus and disrespect the Bible he based his life on.

The Living Word and the written Word vibrated to the same harmonic frequency.

They were both tuned to the same Heart of Love.

The Bible and Love

The heart of the biblical message is that God loves people because of who and what *he* is, not because of who and what *we* are. We do not make God love us. His love existed in his own heart long before we do anything to draw it out from him. "God is love" even if "I am bad."

Whew!

Jesus crafted a story about a boy who cheated his dad and ran away from home as far as his reprobate legs could carry him. In that far-away place, he blasted through every moral boundary his father ever taught him and maxed out every credit card his father ever lent him.

Prodigal means "over the top." This kid is the poster-child for Boys Gone Wild. He was so far out of bounds, even the other partiers in town crossed the street when they saw him coming. "No one would give him anything," said Jesus. No more girls would hop in the sack with him. No more bars would serve him. No more swine-herders would hire him. No more hookers would service him. Not even the sweetest little old lady would let him bum a dime.

He disgusted everyone.

He disgusted himself.

The way Jesus tells the story makes you dislike the prodigal son. And if you can't stand him, just imagine how a holy God feels. Any self-respecting boy-scout would expect God to blast the prodigal son with lighting bolts.

It's at this point that Jesus twisted the plot. When the prodigal pervert was sick enough of drugs, sex, rock-'n-roll, and swine slop, he headed back to the one place he might possibly bum a meal: his father's house.

If this story were in any other religious book, the ending would be wildly different.

In the Muslim *Qur'an*, he would have to repay his father fourfold and have his hand cut off.[10]

In the Buddhist *Sutras*, he would be reincarnated as a deaf mute and have to scale the ladder of perfection from the dirt up.[11]

In the Hindu *Vedas*, he would suffer karmic justice, because what goes around, comes around.[12]

Only in the Bible, with its God of love, can the story end the way Jesus ended it: the loving father has waited daily at the head of the road, longing for his idiot son's return. And when the son does return, his father makes himself a greater idiot by running to him—something no self-respecting nobleman would do in the ancient world.

But Jesus pushes it deeper.

The father not only runs to the pierced, tattooed, lice-ridden, spiked, strung out, STD-risking son, he also embraces him, showers him with kisses, and wastes even more money by throwing a budget-blowing party, complete with a hired band, prime beef on the spit, and dancing.

Love.

The Bible owns it.

Self-giving, self-sacrificing, urgent, passionate, deep love from God's immaculate heart to our putrid souls.

That's my star witness for the truthfulness of the Bible.

What's your verdict?

Love's Mt. Everest

I can't end this line of thought without spotlighting the Bible's Mt. Everest of love: the Cross, where Jesus died. In the story of the prodigal son, the dad calls for the slaughter of the fattened calf. Jesus gives the fattened calf three mentions (Luke 15:23, 27, 30), an often-overlooked factoid. This would be a special calf, culled from the herd, penned near the house, and fed grains and corn. The other cattle ate grass. This one ate grains. It was a *fattened* calf; its whole life was a prelude to death. The family would bond with the calf over time, like a pet, until slaughter-time.

As Jesus crafts his parable, the final party is made possible only by the slaughter of the fattened calf.

Jesus became our fattened calf. He was born to die. He became our sin-bearer on a hill called the Skull (*Calvary*, to use the Latinized name). In the matrix of God's heart, love and justice kissed at the Cross. Christ's shed blood legitimized God's love for prodigals in the face of God's justice against prodigals.

Christ's slaughter makes the celestial party possible. His effort, his work, his sacrifice. Every other religious book demands our effort, our work, our sacrifice. Which makes more sense: the world's religions that say we must reach up to God, or the Bible that insists God has reached down to us? Religion or Grace? Human effort or God's effort? You climbing up or God stooping down?

A life of duty or a life of love?

Which makes more sense?

Really, there are only two religions in the world: the one that has us striving toward God, or the one that has God striving for us through Christ. Christ's sacrifice makes the celestial party possible.

You're invited. Have you delivered your R.S.V.P.?

"Behold what manner of love the Father has bestowed on us, that we should be called children of God!" (1 John 3:1).

------ # & ! $ # + % ----

Talking Points

1. Ask your friends if they believe in a loving God. If they say yes, ask why.

Then ask them to prove it. On the basis of whatever sacred book they believe, make them prove that their divine being majors in love. They won't be able to. Point out that, when it comes to divine love, the Bible is in a league of its own.

2. Discuss the idea of faith as "confidence in an authority," and probe to discover your friend's authority.

If you are a Christian, you submit your mind to the Bible. The Bible becomes your external, objective authority for faith and life. But what if the Bible isn't your authority? Then what? That's what you want to find out with your friends. Where do they get their truth? How do they know what they know about God?

I'll bet your friends *make up* their idea of God, like a little girl dresses her Barbie dolls. It's all about personal preference. Once you dig enough to get your friend to admit it, ask how it feels to be superior to God. After all, anyone who defines God must be better than God, right? Ask if they're comfortable risking their life and eternity on a subjective position they developed because it feels good to them. Then be quiet and let them sweat.

3. Bookmark some websites that deal with so-called Bible discrepancies.

You can find links at www.FourLetterWords.org/word. One of the most common arguments against the Bible is that it is full of mistakes, inconsistencies, and contradictions. In truth, it isn't. But

you'll still have to answer the objection. Rather than memorize a bunch of arguments, it might be easier to get familiar with some websites that have answered, case by case, the most common ones. It helped me a lot to know that, even if I couldn't answer every objection, someone could and has, and I just need to know where to find their answers. Here's a QR code for a website with some really helpful links.

4. Use the Bible in your conversations.

I've had two eerily similar experiences, years apart. In each case, I had spent months debating Jesus-stuff with a friend. We went back and forth and I got frustrated. The first experience was with my antagonistic friend, Raymond. Raymond weighed about 220 pounds in high school. He put forth a scary-violent persona, but I knew he was relatively harmless. He scoffed at my Christianity whenever he had a chance. I argued back.

One day, we sat at lunch, arguing as usual, and it struck me we were rehashing old arguments. It suddenly felt crazy.

So I said, "Raymond, I can't answer all your arguments, but I do know this: 'For God so loved the world that he gave his only begotten Son...'" Then I rattled off a string of Bible verses that I had memorized in Sunday School. No commentary. No argumentation. Just Bible verses. About six of them.

Raymond's reaction was immediate: he got quiet, put his elbows on the table, plopped his head in his hands, and rubbed his head hard, like I was hurting him. Afterwards, Raymond was finished talking with me. He never brought up God again.

Fast-forward five or six years to an evening coffee with Rob. Rob was skinny and intense. After a month of Jesus-talk with Rob, I remembered my Raymond-experience. So I tried it again; I quoted Bible verses to Rob. Rob had exactly the same reaction as Raymond: he got quiet and rubbed his head like I was hurting him. I was mildly freaked out.

So was Rob. He embraced Jesus that night.

I learned a valuable lesson: there's power in God's Word. Intrinsic power. My arguments are just okay, but God's Word is "living and powerful" (Hebrews 4:12). Pardon the illustration, but suppose I were a crook, pointing a gun at you, and you argued, "That's not a real gun—it's a squirt gun..." How long do you think we'd argue before I pulled the trigger?

The Bible is self-authenticating. God loaded it with his own power, beauty, and love.

Pull the trigger.

------ # & ! $ # + % ----

CLICK IT: www.FourLetterWords.org/word

SCAN IT:

powered by BWSCAN.com

CHAPTER 8

*The vague and tenuous hope that God is too kind to
punish the ungodly has become a deadly opiate
for the consciences of millions.*[1]
A.W. TOZER

------ # & ! $ # + % ----

Touchy Ideas

1. Hell is real.
2. God's justice and God's love exist in perfect harmony; therefore, the teaching of Hell in no way contradicts the loving heart of God.
3. Love can't win if holiness loses.
4. A person's response to Jesus in this lifetime determines his or her destiny in the next lifetime.
5. This destiny is permanent and unchanging; Scripture describes no post-mortem second chances.

Touchy Scriptures

1. And as it is appointed for men to die once, but after this the judgment. (Hebrews 9:27)
2. Because He has appointed a day on which He will judge the world in righteousness by the Man whom He has ordained. He has given assurance of this to all by raising Him from the dead. (Acts 17:31)
3. But in accordance with your hardness and your impenitent heart

you are treasuring up for yourself wrath in the day of wrath and revelation of the righteous judgment of God. (Romans 2:5)

4. And anyone not found written in the Book of Life was cast into the lake of fire. (Revelation 20:15)

5. And this is the testimony: that God has given us eternal life, and this life is in His Son. He who has the Son has life; he who does not have the Son of God does not have life. (1 John 5:11, 12)

------ # & ! $ # + % ----

I N RESEARCHING THIS CHAPTER, I stumbled upon some ultra-disturbing statements. In these statements, famous leaders of church history celebrate the damnation of lost people. In the interests of full disclosure, here are some horrid examples.

I apologize in advance.

- *Tertullian, pastor, author, (A.D. 160-220).* "At that greatest of all spectacles, that last and eternal judgment how shall I admire, how laugh, how rejoice, how exult, when I behold so many proud monarchs groaning in the lowest abyss of darkness..."[2]

- *Jonathan Edwards, pastor (1703-1758).* "[T]he sight of hell torments will exalt the happiness of the saints forever... [I]t will really make their happiness the greater..."[3]

- *Samuel Hopkins, pastor (1721-1803).* "This display of the divine character will be most entertaining to all who love God, will give them the highest and most ineffable pleasure. Should the fire of this eternal punishment cease, it would in a great measure obscure the light of heaven, and put an end to a great part of the happiness and glory of the blessed."[4]

"Entertaining?" Are you kidding? Grab your popcorn, and I'll race you for a front row seat to watch the torment of the damned?

If this reflects the spirit of Christ, count me out.

The premise of this book is that Christianity is the most plausible, coherent, and beautiful system ever offered the world. But this "I ♥ Hell" theology spoils that beauty like a stink bomb in an elevator.

The Bible does not whoop it up over hell. Jesus wept over the lostness of people (Luke 19:41). St. Paul wished he could accept damnation himself in place of his countrymen (Romans 9:3). God is not willing that any should perish, declared Peter (2 Peter 3:9). No damnation "happy feet" in sight.

The celebration of hell perverts biblical Christianity. As a pastor and a follower of Jesus, I apologize if this creepy teaching has ever messed with your mind. I'm sorry.

Yes, we have our share of nut-job God-defenders, picketing their hate, but this attitude does not reflect the majority of Christ's followers today. None of the churches, seminaries, or organizations I've been a part of has ever fanned the flames of hell. In fact, the opposite is true. The idea of hell has only prompted sadness and concern among the Jesus-followers I've known.

> MY HEART IS FILLED WITH BITTER SORROW AND UNENDING GRIEF FOR MY PEOPLE, MY JEWISH BROTHERS AND SISTERS. I WOULD BE WILLING TO BE FOREVER CURSED --CUT OFF FROM CHRIST!--IF THAT WOULD SAVE THEM.
> (ROMANS 9:2,3, NLT)

In the mid-nineteenth century, a refined, highly-educated London preacher named R.W. Dale encouraged a rough, uneducated American evangelist named D.L. Moody. Moody conducted a preaching tour in England, and many of the snooty British pastors boycotted him. Dale, however, joined forces with Moody. He said, "Moody is the only preacher who has the right to preach on Hell, because he can't do it without tears in his eyes."

The Bible's revelation of Hell should melt your heart. Divine justice should cause silent awe, not giddy happiness. When Jesus unleashes the forces of judgment in the future apocalypse, the universe responds with stunned silence, not clap-happy glee (Revelation 8:1).

If you're doing a slow burn right now, I get it. For some, even the idea of hell seems obscene. And, nobody can prove heaven, hell, or an afterlife. Like everything else we're talking about, it's a matter of faith. I'm just asking if it's a plausible faith. I think it is, and I'd like to explain why. Right after we explore five hellish viewpoints that wave the "Christian" banner.

Five Views on Hell

1. Universalism, a.k.a., Pluralism

Universalists believe all will be saved through sincere devotion to the religion of their culture, choice, or upbringing. Under this view, Christ is not the only way to God. All roads lead to heaven, like hiking trails converging on the same mountaintop. Universalists claim scriptural support in verses that say God desires "all" people to be saved (1 Timothy 2:4) and that God reconciled "the world" to himself (2 Corinthians 5:19). For them, the character of God begins and ends with love.

In their world, God's love wins, even at the expense of his other attributes of holiness, purity, and truth.

Carlton Pearson, a prominent pastor in the United Church of Christ, said he did not believe "God would consign countless souls—or anyone, for that matter—to hell." He teaches a "gospel of inclusion" which he describes as "basic universalism."[5]

My Inner Nice Guy wants to be a Universalist. No hellfire. No smoldering brimstone. No four letter words hurled my narrow way. No knots to unravel about why I was born in a Christian land and some jungle guy wasn't. It doesn't matter. The story of humankind is one, gigantic happily ever after.

You'll find universalism in churches that call themselves Unity, Universalist, or Unitarian. It is the unofficial position of what can be called liberal Christianity; segments within mainstream groups like some Methodists, Episcopalians, or the United Church of Christ tilt toward Universalism. So do some Ivy League seminary professors, populist authors, many leading institutions of Western civilization—arts, media, education—and celebrities like Oprah.

Warning: from here on, the names get extra confusing. Sorry. I didn't make them up.

2. Universalistic Inclusivism

If my Inner Nice Guy wants to be a universalist, my Inner Conflict Avoider wants to be a universalistic inclusivist. That way I find salvation in Jesus alone and still unclench my hell muscles without losing my evangelical street cred. How does that work?

Universalistic inclusivism works by creating a nifty category called "Anonymous Christians." Under this view, salvation comes through Jesus Christ alone, but people can be saved by Jesus Christ without knowing him by name. Sincere non-Christians benefit from the work of Christ just as much as Christians. Their sincerity proves their "implicit faith."[6]

Sounds like a win/win situation.

The Catholic Church tilted hard this way in the mid-1960's in an epic update called Vatican II. It said,

> Those [who have not yet received the gospel] also can attain to everlasting salvation who through no fault of their own do not know the gospel of Christ or His Church, yet sincerely seek God and, moved by grace, *strive by their deeds* [emphasis added] to do His will as it is known unto them through the dictates of conscience.[7]

This position appears so win/win, in fact, it's also called, "Lenient inclusivism." Who wouldn't want both sides of that label?

If you're looking for universalistic inclusivism, check out your radically up-to-date nearby Catholic church. Also visit some non-Catholic churches formerly known as "emerging," i.e., younger, hipper churches influenced by popular authors like Spencer Burke,[8] Brian McLaren,[9] and Chuck Smith Jr.[10]

3. Universalistic Exclusivism

A good-hearted group of friends began attending my church. They volunteered to duplicate audio and print media for our ministry. They were fun people. As I got to know them, they explained how they had spent most of their lives in a cult, and that their whole cult repented of their false teachings, and came to Jesus.

That got my attention.

Their former church had earned the cult merit badge by claiming Jesus but denying his deity, denying the Trinity, and imposing unusual requirements like triple-tithing, annual pilgrimages, and a lot of legalistic add-ons to the Bible.

My new friends explained how the cult's leadership realized they were messed up, and in one bold move, sent out videos to be played on the same day in all their churches around the world. In that video, they affirmed the classic understanding of Jesus – as God and human in one person, and as the world's only Savior. They affirmed the Trinity and realigned themselves with the historic Christian faith. They apologized for a generation of false teaching, and redirected their organization to the biblical Christian mainstream.

I listened, spellbound. I couldn't recall a single parallel in church history.

The one holdover from their old belief-system, however, was that after death, a person has another chance to receive Jesus. Here is how that group still states it on their website:

> Therefore we can believe that one way or another he urges every person who ever lived, or who ever will live, to trust in him for salvation—whether before they die, at the point of death, *or even after they are dead* [emphasis added]. If some people in the last judgment turn to Christ in faith when they at last learn what he has done for them, then he will certainly not turn them away.[11]

Rob Bell seems to wave this flag in his controversial book, *Love Wins*. He argues, "No one can resist God's pursuit forever because God's love will eventually melt even the hardest hearts."[12]

This would be sweet, if it could pass the Bible's sniff test because you could call Jesus the world's only Savior, but still claim that all will be saved.

This viewpoint is called "exclusivism" because it offers salvation *exclusively* through Jesus. It's called "universalistic" because just about everybody will get saved. After all, with the pearly gates beckoning you forward, and the fires of hell scorching your behind, odds are super-strong you'll become a Jesus-believer fast. Death doesn't close the door on evangelism. Everybody gets a second chance.

You can satisfy your universalistic, exclusivistic, second chance cravings by visiting any church in the Grace Communion International. Noted theologian Clark Pinnock has also advocated this view.[13]

4. Annihilationism

I'm sitting in a coffee shop near a massive, indoor water park called *Great Wolf Lodge,* in Washington State. It's a Mecca for families with kids, so here we are. The heart of Great Wolf Lodge is a massive play structure that shoots water in every direction. A gigantic bucket balances precariously at its top, slowly filling with water. Every five minutes or so, the bucket tips over, dousing brave children with 1,000 gallons of icy water.

My eight-year-old daughter races to stand in the path of the downpour. I stood in the spill-zone just once: it felt like getting pummeled with padded fists, a perfect metaphor for parenthood.

It's also a metaphor for where this analysis of hell is headed. I'm feeling a growing angst as I write because universalism makes me feel good, and I imagine it might make you feel good, too... and we both know I'm just setting us all up for a gigantic bucket of theological cold water.

So, here's fair warning: the bucket is almost full, and it's about to tip. If that makes you want to wing this book, and me, across the room, go ahead (the book, I mean, not me). It won't change the fact that eternal destinies shouldn't be left up to feelings.

Joining the ranks of feel-good tendencies is Annihilationism. My Chicago public high school inflicted enough Latin on my tender brain for me to know that *nihil* means "nothing." To annihilate means "to turn into nothing." Under this view, a person who rejects God through Jesus simply gets erased. God flips a switch, and that

Theories of Universalism/Particularism

FOUR LETTER WORDS
BILL GIOVANNETTI

UNIVERSALISM/ PLURALISM
the teaching that all will be saved, or at least can be saved through sincere devotion to the religion of their culture, choice, or upbringing. Christ is not the only way to God; all sincere roads can lead to God.

UNIVERSALISTIC EXCLUSIVISM
the teaching that all will come to believe in Jesus, either in this life or the next. This is called "second chance" teaching, and it assumes that after death, a person has another chance to receive Jesus.

PARTICULARISM/ EXCLUSIVISM
the teaching that faith alone in Christ alone BY NAME is the only way to God or heaven. Most evangelical institutions are Exclusivistic in the message of salvation.

UNIVERSALISTIC INCLUSIVISM
the teaching that salvation is only through Christ, but that many may be saved without knowing Christ by name...
"Anonymous Christians"
"Implicit Faith"

ANNIHILATIONISM
the teaching that the conscious existence of people who never accept Jesus simply ceases to exist after death. They are annihilated, and do not spend eternity in conscious punishment.

"All roads lead to God"

"Salvation by faith in Jesus by name/identity alone"

person's soul gets shut down, like decommissioning a nuclear reactor.

The flames of hell get doused with cold water, and the wicked take an everlasting nap.

I've also heard this view linked with concepts like "soul sleep"—based on the biblical figure of speech, which uses sleep to speak of death—and "conditional immortality"[14]—based on the idea that your soul is only immortal on the *condition* that you receive Jesus as your Savior. Dying without Jesus automatically triggers your shutdown sequence without further action on the part of God. Humans are mortal until they receive Jesus.[15]

No matter what you call it, annihilationism steps away from universalism. Under this view, not all roads lead to God and not all religions lead to heaven. You still need Jesus; annihilationists do not propose universal salvation.

Nor do they propose eternal damnation in the traditional sense. In their teaching, you die, meet your maker, flunk the cosmic test, and take a nap forever.

Annihilationists point to Bible verses that promise the destruction of the wicked (Philippians 3:19, 1 Thessalonians 5:3, 2 Peter 3:7). Jesus told us to fear God, who has the power "to destroy both soul and body in hell" (Matthew 10:28). Even that world-famous verse, John 3:16, teaches that unbelievers *perish*; they don't *languish*, the argument goes.

Evangelical heavyweights like John Stott have weighed in on the side of conditional immortality. Stott writes,

> I find the concept [of eternal conscious punishment] intolerable and do not understand how people can live with it without either cauterizing their feelings or cracking under the strain.[16]

You can hop into the pool of annihilationism, conditional immortality, and/or soul sleep in churches that have Adventist[17] in their names, in cult-groups like the Jehovah's Witnesses, and in authors like Clark Pinnock and John Stott.

Okay, pop open your umbrella in three, two, one...

5. Particularism, (a.k.a. Exclusivism)

Some people go to heaven, some people go to hell, and what you do with Jesus in this life makes the difference. That's the colossal Christian vexation in a nutshell. A close friend told my wife, "Based on your teachings, you believe I'm going to hell, and that bothers me." Ouch. It bothers my wife and me, too. Exclusivism offends, like scratch-'n-sniff skunk spray.

This view is often called *particularism*, because it defines which particular people go to heaven or hell—not in the sense of certain individuals being predestined for heaven, but of a certain class of people who go to each place. It's called exclusivism, because it excludes people without Jesus from heaven forever. Most mainstream Christian groups have advocated particularism since the days of Jesus himself.

It can be hard to stomach, though. Comedian George Carlin offered this devastating parody of particularism:

> Religion has actually convinced people that there's an invisible man – living in the sky – who watches everything you do, every minute of every day. And the invisible man has a special list of ten things he does not want you to do. And if you do any of these ten things, he has a special place, full of fire and smoke and burning and torture and anguish, where he will send you to live and suffer and burn and choke and scream and cry forever and ever till the end of time... But he loves you![18]

Is defending particularism defending the indefensible?

It depends on how we frame our questions. If we ask, "Is hell real?" we'll have one kind of discussion. But if we ask, "Does the Bible teach that hell is real?" we'll have a whole different conversation. Neither empiricists nor rationalists have the tiniest clue about what happens after we die. All we can do is shout guesses at each other, unless...

Unless we have a credible authority that lifts the veil off this otherwise hidden realm. Jesus-people find that authority in the Bible.

I would like to appeal for some tolerance right now. Please let me make my case. You have the power—you've always had the power—to agree or disagree. But give me a chance. My goal isn't to convince you I'm right. My goal is to convince you that I'm consistent with the Bible and with Jesus. And that the Bible's view meshes seamlessly with the kind of logic already woven deep in our hearts.

What if Hell is Not Real?

What happens to the universe, and our lives, if we subtract hell from the cosmic equation?

1. If hell is not real, then the Christian missionary movement has been a monumental waste of lives and resources.

For two thousand years, the driving force behind Christianity has been Jesus' command: "Go into all the world and preach the gospel to every creature" (Mark 16:15). Christ's followers call this the "Great Commission." In his next statement, Jesus bottom-lined why this was the church's Prime Directive: "He who believes and is baptized will be saved; but he who does not believe will be condemned" (Mark 16:16).

For two thousand years, innumerable Jesus-followers have paid a price so that their friends and neighbors might not be "condemned." The price has been paid in love, sacrifice, service, money, and martyrdom.

If hell is not real, why did Jesus threaten condemnation for those who neglected his gospel? Why did he send his followers on a fools' errand? Why did his earliest followers volunteer to be thrown to lions and burned at the stake rather than ignore the call to world evangelization?

If all roads lead to God (Universalism)...

...or if sincere faith in any name leads to life (Universalistic Inclusivism)...

...or if people can be saved post-mortem (Universalistic Exclusivism)...

...or if unbelieving souls cease to exist after death (Annihilationism)...

...then why did Jesus trigger an avalanche of self-sacrificial evangelism that continues to this day? To throw out hell is to throw out two thousand years of Christian missionary effort and make it colossal nonsense.

And I know that a lot people would nod their heads, thinking *It is colossal nonsense... all of it! Evangelism, hell, condemnation, heaven.* I get that, but any reasonable person has to admit that Christians who believe in hell are consistent with a plain reading of the Bible.

2. If hell is not real, then two thousand years of Christian theology have been mistaken.

There is an unbroken chain of teaching on hell from the first days of Christianity to today. Every generation of Christians has preached the message that those who do not embrace Jesus will go to hell. Here are two famous preachers from the age of Christianity that followed the apostles:

- Justin Martyr (A.D. 151): "[Jesus] shall come from the heavens in glory with his angelic host, when he shall raise the bodies of all the men who ever lived. Then he will clothe the worthy in immortality; but the wicked, clothed in eternal sensibility, he will commit to the eternal fire, along with the evil demons."[19]

- Tertullian (A.D. 197): "After the present age is ended he will judge his worshipers for a reward of eternal life and the godless for a fire equally perpetual and unending."[20]

I'm just showing that Christ's earliest interpreters understood him and his apostles to teach hell without an off-switch.

In his classic study of the history of evangelism, Michael Green examined the earliest generations of the church. He wanted to know what inspired such a radical devotion to spread the fame of Jesus. Green concluded:

> On whether men declare themselves for [Jesus] or against Him depends their eternal destiny. Entry into the kingdom of God depends upon relationship with [Jesus]. Always we meet this religious dualism. It is one of the most objectionable elements in the gospel to modern man. No doubt it was to men of the first century. The scandal of Christ's particularity has always been the supreme obstacle to Christian commitment. But those early Christians believed implicitly that Jesus was the only hope for the world, the only way to God for the human race.[21]

The earliest followers of Jesus got the message. They stuck out as particularists in a pluralist world. Their neighbors thought they were nuts. But it didn't matter. They took Jesus at his word, and turned the world upside down.

If they were wrong, then Christianity has been off-track since the beginning.

3. If hell is not real, then Jesus misled his followers.

Jesus spoke about hell more than any other person in the Bible. He said:

- And do not fear those who kill the body but cannot kill the soul. But rather fear Him who is able to destroy both soul and body in hell. (Matthew 10:28)
- Serpents, brood of vipers! How can you escape the condemnation of hell? (Matthew 23:33)
- Enter by the narrow gate; for wide is the gate and broad is the way that leads to destruction, and there are many who go in by it. Because narrow is the gate and difficult is the way which leads to life, and there are few who find it. (Matthew 7:13,14)

For Hell, Jesus used the Aramaic term *Gehenna*, originally a reference to the smoldering garbage dump outside the walls of Jerusalem. People in Jesus' day believed this valley lay over underground fires. The wicked would be gathered there, they thought, and the earth would open up and swallow them, as it did to the followers of Korah who rebelled against Moses (Numbers 16:30).

Over time, the meaning of Gehenna shifted from the garbage dump to the place of everlasting judgment. When Jesus spoke of Gehenna, his listeners knew what he meant: final judgment, not the town dump.[22]

The offensiveness of Jesus didn't stop with hell-talk, it got worse. Jesus made hell personal. He made a relationship with *himself* the deciding factor in whether or not a person went there. To Jesus, heaven and hell weren't about religions, rituals, correctness, morality, or deeds. They were about a person's faith in Jesus himself. All the writers of the Bible read from the same script: they promised heaven for people who had Jesus and hell for people who didn't.[23]

I'm only echoing the ancient wisdom of biblical sages:

- Jesus said to him, "I am the way, the truth, and the life. No one comes to the Father except through Me." (John 14:6; see also Matt 7:21-23)

- And this is the testimony: that God has given us eternal life, and this life is in His Son. He who has the Son has life; he who does not have the Son of God does not have life. (1 John 5:11-12)

- He who believes in [Jesus] is not condemned; but he who does not believe is condemned already, because he has not believed in the name of the only begotten Son of God. (John 3:18)

In Bible math, (Jesus) = (heaven) and (no Jesus) = (hell).

It's unfair, however, to paint Jesus as a heartless beast. He was heartbroken and angry over the stubbornness that kept people from faith. Jesus grieved over people's lostness (Matt 23:37). He felt their lostness so deeply he urged his followers to the ends of the earth to summon all people to faith in him.

Insistently.

Passionately.

Urgently.

He said, "Go out into the highways and hedges, and compel them to come in, that my house may be filled" (Luke 14:23). Compel them, he said. Don't take no for an answer unless you have to.

No wonder, after Jesus went up to heaven, Peter preached: "Nor is there salvation in any other, for there is no other name under heaven given among men by which we must be saved" (Acts 4:12).

4. If hell is not real, then the universe has no final solution for evil, the Supreme Being is not holy, and Christ's death was an epic waste of a beautiful life.

Some time ago, I built a deck on my patio and needed a permit. At that time, the City of Chicago issued all building permits from one central office. So, off I went, drawings in hand, to stand in line. I had no clue about the hellish lines in the Chicago permit office. It wrapped around the office and stretched into the hallway. As I chatted with fellow line-standers, I learned that builders actually hired people to stand in line for them, because Chicago line-standing is an all-day affair. I was surrounded by professional line-standers.

A couple of foot-shuffling hours later, I neared the Promised Land. I could see the counter where busy clerks issued permits. That's when I noticed the most despicable life-forms on earth: line-jumpers. A well-dressed permit-seeker cut to the front of the line and tied up a clerk, preventing the person in front of me from getting helped.

Something inside me boiled, but I held it in (I'm a pastor, so I get paid to not explode). Moments later, it happened again. A guy in blue jeans cut in line, and tied up the next free clerk. My clerk. My reward after hours of waiting. I cracked.

"Hey buddy," I yelled. "The line starts back there, in the hallway." My thumb pointed the way.

Have you ever been line-jumped? Maybe at Costco or Sam's Club or Disney World? the grocery store?

How does it feel?

To me, it felt hot, like sunburn. I hate injustice. Don't you?

When I yelled at the line-jumper, my professional line-waiting friends shushed me, explaining that the clerks sent applicants to different departments for various stamps, and then brought them back to the front of the line to pick up their permits.

My red-faced embarrassment felt hot, too.

Even so, think about how you felt the last time someone cut in front of you. Or the last time someone treated you unfairly. If you're like most people, you have an instinctive response. You say, "That's not fair! The line starts back there."

Where does that instinct for fairness come from? Christians say it comes from God. It is a universal trait. Every society has a sense of justice. Christians think this is a faint reflection of the tarnished image of God within us.

If we imperfect humans have a sense of justice, how much more does our perfect God have a sense of justice too? I'm not saying I can prove it; I'm just saying it makes sense.

God's justice is the ultimate reason for hell. If God were not just, there would be no hell. Evil would create no imbalance in the universe that needed divine correction. Everyone from axe-murderers to genocidal Hitlers to child abusers would get off totally free. Evil would win in the end.

Isn't it true that if divine righteousness does nothing, evil wins?

Consider the alternative to hell: do you really want to live in a universe where evil goes unpunished? Imagine a universe where the Supreme Being accepts evil or tolerates it. Imagine a universe where God is indifferent to evil, cruelty, or abuse. Do you really want that kind of God or that kind of universe?

You might say, "No, I don't. I do want God to punish evil. I just don't want him to punish it so *severely*. Must there be fire? Must it last forever? Why such a hellish hell?"

Hold that thought and consider this: if you want God to punish evil – even a little – then you want some form of hell. Whether it's in this life, or the next; whether it's hot or not; whether it's temporary or eternal. You want some form of hell, because if you don't, you don't want goodness to win in the end. Most people are pro-hell; they just want a kinder, gentler hell.

We instinctively know divine love can't win if divine holiness loses. What if God simply will not make war in his own character to make peace with us?

If you were constructing a universe, and really thinking about it, you would construct a universe in which God was holy, and the moral line-jumpers of the cosmos got punished. Any other universe would be intolerable. That is why the Bible makes so much sense: it echoes our heart's deepest instincts.

Hell means that evil has a far-away parking place, and God is fair forever. The bad guys get away with nothing. The force that hurt you, the person who exploited you, and the powers that consumed you, get their due. Hell proves that God takes it personally when people hurt people (sin); he doesn't just yawn and scratch his armpit.

If you're evil's victim (and you are), you might take comfort in that.

If you're evil's perpetrator (and you are), you might find terror in that.

Welcome to the biblical worldview.

Enter Jesus who solved both sides of evil's equation. He took the hit for evil's perpetrators that he might liberate evil's victims. He endured, in three dark hours on the Cross, the infinity of God's wrath against evil. He absorbed the hell we deserved, legitimizing the heaven we don't deserve. He entered the cage match against evil, and won by a knockout. He made it legit for a sinless God to welcome sinful people into his company. God can express his love without erasing his justice. So the Bible can promise: "So now there is no condemnation for those who belong to Christ Jesus" (Romans 8:1, NLT). The question God wants echoed over every rooftop is do you belong to Christ Jesus?

So, this is me, echoing God's question to you: do you belong to Christ Jesus?

The Father's Heart

I'm haunted by a true-life story I heard from Todd Adams, a missionary in Africa. He was driving over bouncy African roads when he stopped for an unexpected road-block. Out of nowhere, his jeep was car-jacked by local thugs. They threw open his door, dragged him from the vehicle, and flung him to the ground. Todd watched as his vehicle sped off.

powered by BWSCAN.com

Todd's two little kids were buckled in the back seat.

TODD ADAMS'S STORY, MP3

Words can't describe the feeling of that moment. Todd told how the now distant jeep was suddenly forced to make a U-turn, racing back toward him, presenting his one and only chance. He sprinted toward the jeep as it sped past, and jumped to grab the outside-mounted spare tire. He held on for dear life. As the jeep bounced across the pitted road, Todd clambered to plant his feet on the back bumper. He slapped a death-grip on the roof rack. That's when he saw his kids inside.

They were crying and screaming for Daddy. His heart was shattered. The car-jackers knew Todd was on the back and tried to shake him loose.

Todd wouldn't let go.

Todd refused to let go.

He had a father's heart.

Todd's story had a happy ending. The car-jackers got more than they bargained for, stopped the jeep, and fled on foot. Todd gathered his children into his arms and embraced them like never before.

His words still haunt me. "If you don't understand how urgently God wants his lost children found, then you don't understand your Father's heart."

Do not let your idea of hell eclipse the splendor of God's love. The greatest logical difficulty is not that there should be a hell, but that there should be a heaven, and that moral misfits should populate it. Logic can't explain it. Religion can't create it. Human effort can't merit it. Only the Bible's God can accomplish it.

Heaven can only be the free gift of God's love, courtesy the blood of God's Son. Like any gift, it must be accepted.

Received.

Taken by faith.

Can I prove it? No. Does it ring true? It does for me. How about you?

Do you belong to Jesus?

------ # & ! $ # + % ----

Talking Points

1. In the Bible, God's followers showed respect for the people of other cultures, but blanket disrespect for their religions and gods.

Though God's people respected people of other nationalities – their law required kindness for visitors from other cultures (Exodus 22:21, 23:9) – they rejected their neighbor's religions. No matter how long you scan the Bible's horizons, you'll never find a glimmer of religious pluralism that gains God's stamp of approval.

- Paul was respectful of the Athenians as people, though he called their religious views "ignorant" (Acts 17:16-34).

- God's prophet, Elijah, mocked the priests of the god, Baal and called people to choose between the true God and false gods (1 Kings 18:21-40).

- King David called gods of the other nations "demons" (Psalm 106:35-37).

- When God's people conquered idol worshipping cities, they were to completely destroy their religions artifacts: "But thus you shall deal with them: you shall destroy their altars, and break down their sacred pillars, and cut down their wooden images, and burn their carved images with fire." (Deuteronomy 7:5).

- St. Paul echoed David when he claimed that everybody who worships an idol is really worshipping a "demon" (an evil spirit, 1 Corinthians 10:21).

In fact, the Bible forbids any morphing of Christianity with other religions.

This does not mean we should run around rebuking false religious views and damning people to hell. It means we hold our convictions passionately and, through love and truth, attract our friends and neighbors to Jesus.

2. Though hell is real, it is not God's Plan A for any person.

God doesn't want people to go to hell. "Indeed," Jesus says, "God did not send His Son into the world to condemn the world but in order that the world" – every single human being – "might be saved through Him" (John 3:17). Peter preached, "The Lord is not willing that any should perish but that all"—every single human being—"should come to repentance" (2 Peter 3:9). Paul describes

God's heartfelt desire: "For this is good and acceptable in the sight of God our Savior, who desires all men to be saved and to come to the knowledge of the truth" (1 Timothy 2:3-4).

On your best day you can't imagine how passionately God loves every human being and desires each one's company in heaven forever.

Then why does anybody go to hell?

3. God takes human freedom with infinite seriousness.

God will not cram salvation down anybody's throat. You are free to believe, and free not to believe, in Jesus. John Hannah said,

> No one who is ever in hell will be able to say to God, "You put me here," and no one who is in heaven will ever be able to say, "I put myself here." Salvation is offered to "whoever wills" (Revelation 22:17).[25]

People are in hell only because they have chosen against God (John 3:36).

G.K. Chesterton said, "Hell is God's great compliment to the reality of human freedom and the dignity of human personality."[26]

Your friend might bring up two objections: 1) Doesn't the vast array of world religions prove that people are choosing *for* God to the best of their abilities? and, 2) Should tribal villagers on remote islands be condemned for never hearing of Jesus?

1) No, and, 2) no, and here's why.

4. Humans are universally guilty of disrespecting the "Godness" of God the Father.

Nothing offends non-Christians more than the preaching of an exclusive gospel. How can a loving God damn someone to hell for being born into a jungle tribe that had no knowledge of Jesus? Isn't that unfair?

Yes, it's unfair, and that's why God doesn't do it.

You read it right. God doesn't condemn people to hell just because they never heard of Jesus.

He condemns them because they've heard of God the Father and rejected him first.

Their idols prove it.

Any thinking person who contemplates the night sky and the wonders of nature spends at least a few moments wondering where it all came from. Even the most isolated villager in the most primitive tribe has a story of a Supreme Being who is bigger than the material universe. God has left enough fingerprints on creation to spark a quest for him in every human heart. Sooner or later everybody "pings" God – like a sonar operator searching for a submarine.

The Bible says,

> For the truth about God is known to them [the whole world] instinctively. God has put this knowledge in their hearts. From the time the world was created, people have seen the earth and sky and all that God made. They can clearly see his invisible qualities—his eternal power and divine nature. So they have no excuse whatsoever for not knowing God (Romans 1:19, 20, NLT).

But as soon as that pinging begins, our Inner Rebel fights back. "I don't want a Big God I can't control," we say. "I want a handy mini-god who does my bidding." This rebellion is universal: we're ALL guilty of it. Whether we reduce God to a manageable idol or park him in the land of fairy tales makes no difference. We abridge the Infinite Creator to a pocket-sized edition. We each become, in effect, our own god and god-maker. This is the core truth of human guilt – not the ignorance of Jesus, but the Great Rebellion against a Father God who shouts his existence from the sky.

What if world religions never did represent a quest for God? What if they have always represented mankind's best effort to *domesticate* God?

St. Paul writes about people who are religious, but who shrink down the Godness of God. He explains how God deals with them: "Yes, they knew God, but they wouldn't worship Him as God or even give Him thanks. And they began to think up foolish ideas of what God was like. The result was that their minds became dark and confused" (Romans 1:21, NLT).

He describes how they turned to idols and how God responds to this choice: "God gave them up" (Romans 1:24, 26, 28). Three times he says it: God gave them up, or as one translation puts it, "God let them go ahead and do whatever their shameful hearts desired" (v. 24, NLT).

They rejected God first. So God did the only thing he could do without crushing human freedom: he confirmed them in their choice. The conclusion is, "Therefore you are without excuse" (Romans 1:20; 2:1). *Even those who never heard of Jesus?* Yes, because *everybody* has heard of or thought of God the Father.

Why should the Father tell them of his Son when they've already rejected the Father? If your god is so small that your own efforts can save you, you have already decided you don't need Jesus. Why should God tell you of a Savior if you've pre-decided you don't need one? Or if you've pre-decided you can roll your own? That is your choice. There's no excuse. Not even if you live on an isolated island.

You might not like it, but will you admit the logic makes sense? Will you admit your argument is with the Bible, not with your Jesus-following friend?

5. The Bible indicates there might be degrees of punishment in hell.

Speaking of Judgment Day, Jesus warned cities that rejected his disciples and their gospel message, saying, "It will be more tolerable in that Day for Sodom than for that city" (Luke 10:12; Mark 6:11).

Speaking of people who have a clear knowledge of Christ and reject him anyway, the author of Hebrews warns:

> Of how much worse punishment, do you suppose, will he be thought worthy who has trampled the Son of God underfoot, counted the blood of the covenant by which he was sanctified a common thing, and insulted the Spirit of grace? (Hebrews 10:29).

Peter warns those who flirt with Jesus and then reject him, "the latter end is worse for them than the beginning. For it would have been better for them not to have known the way of righteousness, than having known it, to turn from the holy commandment delivered to them" (2 Peter 2:20,21).

In each case, Judgment Day is said to be worse for some than others. Whatever else this might mean, it means this: *God knows exactly what each person deserves and would never punish more severely than justice allows.* He controls the *way justice feels* with a perfect blend of holiness and grace. When we finally see who's where experiencing what, we will breathe a sigh of relief, and confess that God got it right—it could be no other way. Because God is perfectly just when he speaks and eternally blameless when he judges (Psalm 51:4).

6. Finally, if the idea of hell bothers you, then tell people about Jesus.

Invite people into His kingdom. Love people. Care for people. Serve people. Share your life with people. Above all, let the gospel/good news of Jesus ooze out of your life through words and deeds.

Your corner of the world desperately needs to hear about Jesus Christ; that's why God put you there. I hope Michael Green's observation on evangelism in the early church lights a fire in your belly:

> Now if you believe that outside of Christ there is no hope, it is impossible to possess an atom of human love and kindness without being gripped with a great desire to bring men to this one way of salvation.[27]

------ # & ! $ # + % ----

CLICK IT: www.FourLetterWords.org/damn

SCAN IT:

powered by BWSCAN.com

The deepest problem of our lives, whether heterosexual or homosexual, is the terrible exchange of the glory of God for images. The exchange of the truth of God for a lie... Failed worship is our worst disorder. This is beneath all the maladies of the world. Repairing this, not first our disordered sexuality, is our main business in life.[1]

JOHN PIPER

------ # & ! $ # + % ----

Touchy Ideas

1. Single people shouldn't have sex.
2. Married people shouldn't have sex with a person they're not married to.
3. You don't have to "see if the sex is good" before you get married, because, if you love each other, you can make the sex good.
4. People with a healthy sexuality can and will wait for marriage.
5. Sex creates emotional bonds that can haunt you when you break them.

Touchy Scriptures

1. You shall not commit adultery. (Exodus 20:14)
2. Whoever commits adultery with a woman lacks understanding; He who does so destroys his own soul. (Proverbs 6:32)
3. Marriage is honorable among all, and the bed undefiled; but fornicators and adulterers God will judge. (Hebrews 13:4)
4. Flee sexual immorality. Every sin that a man does is outside the

body, but he who commits sexual immorality sins against his own body. (1 Corinthians 6:18)

5. But I say to you that whoever looks at a woman to lust for her has already committed adultery with her in his heart. (Matthew 5:28)

------ # & ! $ # + % ----

You've probably eaten anti-sex food created by Christians and not known it. In 1829, the Rev. Sylvester Graham launched a movement to reduce the frequency of sex. All varieties of it, even by married couples. There was simply too much lust in his world. The best way to turn down the heat, he figured, was through a bland diet. He concocted the humble cracker that bears his name as the world's first commercial "anti-aphrodisiac."

S'mores anyone?

By the 1890's, Graham's gospel of sexual minimalism caught on. A nutritionist, Dr. John Harvey Kellogg, joined the dietary fray. He preached sexual abstinence and lectured against masturbation – calling it a leading cause of disease and death. The fastest route to a temptation-free life, he taught, was to avoid stimulating food and drink. And so the world's second famous anti-sex food was born in the form of Mr. Kellogg's famous flaked corn cereal.

Will someone please spare Jesus from his followers?

Christians have a well-deserved reputation for weirdness when it comes to sexuality.

The last thing I want to do is feed that misconception. So let me quickly say that Jesus and the authors of Scripture are universally positive about healthy sex lives. For example:

- As a loving deer and a graceful doe, Let her breasts satisfy you at all times; And always be enraptured with her love. (Proverbs 5:19)
- Let your fountain be blessed, And rejoice with the wife of your youth. (Proverbs 5:18)
- Your two breasts are like two fawns, Twins of a gazelle, Which feed among the lilies. (Song of Solomon 4:5)
- Marriage is honorable among all, and the bed undefiled [anything goes that both husband and wife agree to]. (Hebrews 13:4)

Thank God for sex. The idea that sex is bad is not biblical. In fact, the Bible commands a husband and wife to be sexually available to one another as much as possible, so that you don't frustrate your partner into seeking sex elsewhere:

> So do not deprive each other of sexual relations. The only exception to this rule would be the agreement of both husband and wife to refrain from sexual intimacy for a limited time, so they can give themselves more completely to prayer. Afterward they should come together again so that Satan won't be able to tempt them because of their lack of self-control. (1 Corinthians 7:5, NLT)

God is pro-sex. He designed body parts and orgasms. But God does place limits on sex: sex is for a husband and wife who are married to each other. Any other sexual relationship is off limits. He wants us to wait for marriage.

Once again, Christ's followers wind up looking Amish, and our beliefs seem bizarre. We're the inventors of Graham crackers, flaked corn, gender-segregated swimming, and skorts. We are the last puritanical hold-outs in a sexually liberated world.

Our friends ask why they should wait. Why would God make sex so natural, so beautiful, and so pleasurable if he was going to yank it off the table till we're married?

Why would so many cultures around the world define having numerous sex partners as normal?

Don't we believe in sexual liberation?

Please don't consider this chapter an abstinence workshop. It's not. So no paragraphs full of data, and no list of studies to make my case. I'm not so sure I can convince anybody who's sexually active to slam on the brakes, anyway, though veteran NBA player A.C. Green is great at this. Scan the QR code to visit his site if you want help becoming abstinent.

In this chapter, I want to explain why waiting for sex makes sense. I want to applaud virginity until marriage and fidelity within marriage. I want to come alongside those who have preserved their virginity to tell you you've done well, you're not weird, and God is proud of you. And for those who have crossed that line, I want to preach the gospel of secondary virginity, because it's never too late to start over.

Here are four reasons why waiting is a good idea. Like a bullseye, they start at the circumference and move toward the center.

Why Wait?

1. Because God commands it.

The Bible describes sexy stuff because God is cool with sex. The forty-plus authors of Scripture, spanning over 1,500 years of changing culture and politics, never budged from sexuality's Prime Directive: one man, one woman, one lifetime.

Could this be because God was so clear from the beginning: "Therefore a man shall leave his father and mother and be joined to his wife, and they shall become one flesh" (Genesis 2:24)?

Several millennia later, Jesus echoed that original truth:

> And He answered and said to them, 'Have you not read that He who made them at the beginning 'made them male and female,' and said, 'For this reason a man shall leave his father and mother and be joined to his wife, and the two shall become one flesh'? So then, they are no longer two but one flesh. Therefore what God has joined together, let not man separate. (Matthew 19:4-6)

God's brainchild is simple: *one man, one woman, one lifetime.*[2]

You might object that the Bible promotes polygamy (multiple spouses, especially wives). Not really. Scripture never presents polygamy as Plan A. From its first mention in connection with the murderer Lamech (himself a descendent of the murderer Cain), polygamy is almost always associated with negative consequences (Genesis 4:19,23). Like divorce, God let it happen but didn't endorse it. Nothing can ever shake the scriptural ideal of a lifetime union between one man and one woman.

Does that make God a sexually repressed nerd? Is he like a church lady with her hair bun wound so tight her face puckers? No. How could the One who created men to be hard and women to be soft, who loaded our sex organs with pleasure-giving nerve endings, and super-charged us with hormones and pheromones ever be considered a prude?

He created corn, not corn flakes.

There must be a deeper reason for sexual purity than a seemingly arbitrary command from God.

There is.

Another reason to wait is...

2. Because love demands it.

God designed you to love and to be loved. This requires that you know and are deeply known by another flesh and blood human.

What if unmarried sex bypassed true intimacy? What if it spoiled true love?

If you were the celestial lawgiver, and if love were your highest value, what kind of laws would you give about behaviors that not only damaged love, but also damaged our ability to love?

Wouldn't you put up a giant stop sign in front of those behaviors?

God designed sex to bring two people together in the strongest possible bond. When you mess with God's design, you mess with both, a) your bond, and b) your ability to bond. The Bible uses the Greek word *porneia* to refer to sexual activity that crosses God's boundaries. *Porneia* is usually translated "sexual immorality" or "fornication." One Bible commentary says this word describes "every kind of unlawful sexual intercourse." It can include:

- Premarital sex
- Pornography (all kinds including Internet, print, TV, movies, phone sex)
- Sexual addiction behaviors
- "Alternative" sexual lifestyles

- Hooking up
- Multiple sexual partners (in series or all at once)
- Sex for hire
- Perpetrating sexual abuse

All of this is included in the Greek word *porneia*.

My friend, Donny, became a Christian after spending years producing pornography. His life has changed dramatically for the better. He tells a story of a friend named Michael who wanted to help him photograph porn. Donny let him help. After a couple of sessions, Michael quit. He said that photographing porn was ruining his sex life.

Why? Because whatever internal mechanism God gave to churn out intimacy, *porneia* throws sand into it. When a guy masturbates to porn, or a woman hunts down a sex-partner at a bar, the last thing on their minds is *intimacy*. I counseled one sex addict who told me the hardest part of having sex with a lot of different women was kissing them. It felt too intimate, he said.

Think about that. He could insert part A into part B and share orgasms, no problem. But kissing was murder. Why? Because kissing involves knowing. Kissing is face to face, person to person, soul to soul... and *porneia* is its opposite.

Porneia creates only artificial bonds. In fact, *porneia* is both a self-protective and self-indulgent tactic to *avoid* bonding and intimacy. *Porneia* doesn't bring you close to a person; it brings you close to either a body or a computer-enhanced image of a body that exists only in fantasy-land.

Porneia is the instrumental use of sex. In every act, the perpetrator uses another sacred person as an instrument of pleasure. It's about getting *it*, not about loving *her* or *him*. It is sex depersonalized.

Porneia is also the commercial use of sex. This happens when people use sex to get a better job, to be cool, or to obtain drugs or status or money. But sexual love, as God designed it, is not commercial. It is self-giving, self-surrendering, self-sacrificing, and self-disclosing first, and self-satisfying second.

Could that be why Someone far wiser than us cautioned us to save it for the lifelong commitment called marriage?

What if healthy sexuality allowed no such thing as uncommitted love? And what if the only commitment that made sexual love a safe and true love was a lifetime commitment?

You might object that what you feel toward your current partner is indeed true love, and you're insulted that I would make light of it.

I'm not making light of it. I think the feelings we develop toward each other are profound and deeply important. But love involves more than feelings. Love involves the choice to respect yourself as you honor others.

Maybe the question you need to ask yourself is, "Why *not* wait?"

Why not wait till marriage? Why not save yourself for the person willing to make the ultimate commitment? Why not wait until someone vows to live and die for you before opening your soul and body so deeply to that person?

What's the rush?

Let's consider some potential reasons for hopping in the sack before marriage:

- It feels good.
- Everyone does it.
- My friends will think I'm a freak if I don't.
- It's natural, so why not?

- I have needs.
- I'm lonely and I want to know what love is.
- I'll lose my boyfriend/girlfriend.
- I can't control myself.
- We don't need a piece of paper to make it right.
- We're committed to each other.
- I love him/her, so I have to put out.
- He/she loves me, so they'd better put out.

Go back over this list and ask which answers demonstrate a deep and enduring respect for your partner's sacredness. Could it be there are no truly *loving* reasons for sex outside of marriage? What if all of the reasons for *porneia* were either self-centered or dysfunctional?

I'm not trying to dump corn flakes on your sexuality parade. Sex is God's gift. It is, however, such a powerful gift, it can easily backfire if we mess with it.

I'm just suggesting that when you commit the intimate act called sex in a non-intimate manner, it messes with your mind and makes you emotionally numb. True intimacy involves a person's body, emotions, spirit, and mind: all the parts of you, even the non-sexual ones. True intimacy focuses on deeply knowing and deeply being known by one person. Look at little old grandmas and grandpas, caring for each other, holding hands in silence, smiling at each other's jokes, getting teary-eyed at memories of shared heartbreaks and joys.

You will never develop a love that deep if you continually trade partners.

The only love worth giving and receiving—the only love that treats the other person as a precious son or daughter of God—is a love that wraps sex in a lifetime, monogamous commitment called marriage. We wait because true love demands it.

But there's an even deeper reason to wait.

3. Because self-respect requires it.

When you respect sex, you respect yourself.

Your sex life is like an emotional adhesive; it glues you relationally to another person. Premarital sex wears out the adhesive before you get married. Like a Band-Aid that has been ripped off too many times, sex's holding power weakens every time you change partners.

So the Bible says, "Dear friends, I urge you, as aliens and strangers in the world, to abstain from sinful desires, which war against your soul" (1 Peter 2:11, NIV). If you care about your soul, you'll wait.

Your Ideal Heavenly Father, who loves you deeply, counsels you to run away from *porneia* (1 Corinthians 6:18). It deadens your emotions. It can turn you into a machine who churns out sex, but is clueless about intimacy.

It's tough to erase memories of casual sex partners. It's tough to forget pornographic images. These memories travel with you into each new relationship, and adulterate—water down—the strength of your new bond.

Picture your sex drive as a little engine in your heart. When you practice *porneia*, something goes wrong with the little engine. It's as if you've slammed it in reverse. Your sex drive no longer advances you toward intimacy; it pulls you away from intimacy. Your bonder is broken.

That's when your soul initiates any number of five emotion-numbing shifts:

- The shift from feeling emotions to escaping emotions.
- The shift from intimacy to isolation.
- The shift from self-revelation to self-concealment.
- The shift from self-discovery to relational cluelessness.

• The shift from connection to predation.

King Solomon, most likely a recovering sex addict himself, connected the dots between *porneia* and self-respect by describing a young fool hopping in the sack with a seductive woman. Solomon asks, "Can a man scoop fire into his lap and not be burned?" (Proverbs 6:27, NLT). Play with *porneia* and get burned. Solomon adds, "He did not know it would cost his life" (meaning his sense of being fully alive, Proverbs 7:23).

Sexual scatteredness and relational intimacy don't exist inside the same soul.

When you treat sex as sacred, you treat your soul as sacred.

When you respect sex, you respect yourself. That's the third circle in the bullseye. But it's not the real core. Because the central reason to wait is super-simple:

4. Because loyalty to God necessitates it.

Jesus loves you, died for you, shed his blood for you, rose again for you. When you received him, he came to live inside you. Wherever you go, whatever you do, you contain within your skin, the living, powerful life of Christ in you.

And as a Christian, your loyalty to Jesus should outweigh your loyalty to everyone and everything else. That's the bullseye. That's the simple, core message of biblical sexuality. Biblical sexuality is all about loyalty to God, loyalty to Jesus, as a response to his immeasurable loyalty to us.

Jesus said, "You are my friends [loyalty, affection, enjoyment of each other] if you do whatever I command you" (John 15:14).

Why should you wait? Because you are loyal to Jesus. He proved himself infinitely loyal to you; now you can reciprocate that loyalty and prove yourself loyal to him. Have you ever acknowledged your body as a vehicle for the glory of God?

> Flee sexual immorality. Every sin that a man does is outside the body, but he who commits sexual immorality sins against his own body. Or do you not know that your body is the temple of the Holy Spirit who is in you, whom you have from God, and you are not your own? For you were bought at a price; therefore glorify God in your body and in your spirit, which are God's. (1 Corinthians 6:18-20)

Do you glorify God in your body? Are you loyal to Jesus with your body? The more you prove yourself loyal to Jesus, the more you'll gain self worth. The deeper your self worth, the better you'll love others.

Love is the goal, isn't it?

Isn't it?

Advice from a Dad

Today's generations enter puberty with two strikes against them: dysfunctional families and a dysfunctional culture. People of older generations might have grown up in dysfunctional families, but at least they had a largely functional culture. I was reared in a loving, but broken family, ultimately divorced. The Sexual Revolution of the sixties was a new thing, and the more functional Happy Days of the fifties still flexed enough muscle to keep a lot of young people in line, including me.

All that has changed.

When older generations "did it" they didn't brag about it, except in locker rooms and taverns. They kept it secret. Society was organized to favor waiting, especially in the case of women.

Today, that value has been flipped on its head. Premarital sex is not only accepted, it's expected. You're weird if you wait. Social constraints have gone "poof" and sex without boundaries is the new normal. If you're going to remain loyal to God, respectful of yourself, loving toward others, and obedient to God's Word, you need to swim against the current.

I'd like to encourage you in that effort. I'm a dad, I can't help myself. My heart is with you. Picture me on the banks of that river, cheering you on as you swim upstream. Here are some practical pointers to keep you going strong.

1. Understand your herd.

We are herd animals. University researchers conducted an experiment on crowd behavior.[4] Volunteers were told to randomly walk around a large hall without talking to each other. They were essentially clueless as to where to go and what to do. They wandered aimlessly.

A select few were given clear instructions on what path to walk.

The researchers discovered that random wanderers ended up blindly following those who knew where they were going. The tipping point was five percent. In a group of two hundred, just ten informed individuals were able to lead the whole pack, simply by knowing where they were going.

Think of your own peer group. Are you more of a leader or a follower?

If you are a leader, lead the pack to wholeness.

If you are a follower, don't blindly follow the pack off an emotional cliff.

Understand your herd, and switch herds if you must. Pick friends who draw you closer to the life God had in mind for you on the day he saved you. That doesn't mean you should throw people overboard; you shouldn't. It does however mean that your priority must be your own integrity before God.

Campus study groups like Campus Life, InterVarsity, Young Life, church young adult groups, and home-based small groups, offer the peer relationships that will help you in your uphill battle to stay sexually pure.

2. Find a mentor.

Your heavenly Father promised to fill in the gaps left by your earthly father. He calls himself "a father to the fatherless" (Psalm 68:5).

Luke Skywalker had Yoda.

Frodo had Gandalf.

Cinderella had the Fairy Godmother.

Samuel had Eli (1 Samuel 3).

Telemachus had the father-figure, Mentor, in the Greek legend that started this ball rolling.[7]

And you can have whoever God has strategically positioned in your life to mentor you on your journey. These are the men and women who will speak wisdom into your life if you'll let them. They will come and go, but if you position yourself to find them, you will.

Like Yoda, they might not be the coolest kid on the block. Like Gandalf, they might seem old and crotchety. And like the Fairy Godmother, they might be a bit too plump. Don't be picky. You are looking for wisdom, integrity, and love, not a high hipster quotient.

You are looking for a Christ-centered sage willing to drink good coffee with you, speak firm truths to you, and share life with you.

Warning: if you feel creepy about a person, trust your instincts and move on. It might take you a while to connect with the right mentor, but don't give up the search. If you are open to it, they'll find you. God will make sure they find you. Keep your eyes open.

Through the years, God has provided a roster of unlikely heroes in my life: people who mentored me when I didn't realize it. You can read my tribute to them on my blog, at this QR code.

powered by BWSCAN.com

TRIBUTE TO MY MENTORS

While I probably can't mentor you personally, I'd love to play whatever small part in your journey I can. Let's connect at the *Four Letter Words* website and through social media like *Facebook*.

A loving father in your life, or a mentor if your dad isn't quite there enough, is one of the surest indicators you will have the inner strength to swim against the sexual current and to wait.

3. Walk in God's forgiveness.

I've worked with countless young adults and teens who haven't waited and feel crappy about it. One popular college student was crushed to discover he'd been labeled "man whore" by his classmates. He became desperate for a new start.

If you've gone too far, then what?

Then, there's tremendous hope, healing, and forgiveness for you through Christ. You can start over. God shouts his redemptive news on every page of Scripture. Here are two of my favorites. The first one makes sense right away; the second one takes some explaining.

> Come now, and let us reason together," Says the LORD, "Though your sins are like scarlet, They shall be as white as snow; Though they are red like crimson, They shall be as wool. (Isaiah 1:18)

If you're breathing, it's not too late to return to God. He has no "point of no return." He not only erases your guilt, he cleanses your memories, too. Best of all, he promises to never throw your sins in your face—because the Cross of Christ has you covered once for all. You can be white as snow with God. You can start over. Jesus offers good news. Will you embrace it?

Here's the second verse:

> So I will restore to you the years that the swarming locust has eaten, The crawling locust, The consuming locust, And the chewing locust, My great army which I sent among you. (Joel 2:25)

Locusts? Imagine hordes of them gnawing the corners of your conscience, your self-worth, and your identity. Imagine them robbing years of life from you—real life, the life you were meant to live. Now imagine God squashing them, and not only forgiving you, but restoring the wasted years. Only God can make up for lost time. Return to him with your sexuality, and good stuff starts to happen.

I have one last bit of fatherly advice.

4. Prepare for marriage.

Marriage = a lifetime of guilt-free sex, among other benefits. So buck the trend and marry young. The average American male marries at age 27.5 (up from 22.8 in 1960). The average American woman marries at age 25.6 (up from 20.3). Basically, we've postponed marriage for five years.[5] Five years of sexual frustration. Why wait... for marriage?

Don't push it too early, though. Getting married as a teenager triples your chances of divorce.[6]

But getting married older increases your odds of pre-marital sex. Do the math.

I think St. Paul did the math when he counseled, "But if they cannot exercise self-control, let them marry. For it is better to marry than to burn with passion" (1 Corinthians 7:9). It is better to marry, than to fornicate, so prepare for marriage. Get in shape. Get into an honorable dating game. Find a Christ-following partner. Tie the knot. Save sex for your wedding night. Have fun.

God is practical.

You and your partner need at least five healthy factors in place before you even think of getting married: 1) common faith in, and proven dedication to, Jesus; 2) clearly articulated and mutually shared core values; 3) a stable means of financial support without going into debt—don't marry a freeloader; 4) relatively non-dysfunctional, sane, healthy ways of relating (get counseling if you have to, with both partners at least a couple years clean and sober), and 5) enough respect for God, yourselves, and the institution of marriage that you won't go into it with anything less than a lifetime commitment.

A lifetime of guilt-free sex waits at your doorstep. Get married first.

And don't let flaked corn and graham crackers slow you down.

------ # & ! $ # + % ----

Talking Points

1. Sex is spiritual.

Every sex act, real or imagined, involves not just your body, but your soul and spirit too. Every time you commit *porneia* you send messages to your inner being that mess you up in the long run. You create bonds, rip them apart, create new bonds with different partners (or fantasy images), rip them apart, and enter a vicious cycle.

Yeah, it's fun and it feels good.

But the empty feeling after years of messing around doesn't feel good at all. You might pleasure your body, but you'll numb your spirit in the process.

2. God is pro-sex.

God engineered sex for three main reasons: *recreation* (he wants us to have fun and feel good); *procreation* (he wants us to make babies and populate the earth); and *bond-creation* (he want us to form deep bonds of affection and intimacy with a lifetime partner).

God has never been the corn-flake making, graham cracker baking, old maid we've made him out to be. He created orgasms. Enough said.

3. A truly tolerant person would support a Christ-follower's choice to remain abstinent until marriage – without ridicule, pressure, or ostracism.

Just because the sexually permissive tribe has spoken, it shouldn't mean virgins should get kicked off the island. To be sexually abstinent is to be counter-cultural. Welcome to Jesus' world. He bucked every trend that needed bucking—including the sexual permissiveness of the prevailing Roman culture.

I am proud of every young man and woman who waits. Or, if you've already crossed that line, I'm proud of you for crossing back. Secondary virginity takes guts. Anybody on any day can hook up with somebody and have sex. How does that make you special? Every time you wrestle sexual temptation to the ground, and live in the power of God, the angels of heaven cheer, your heart feels cherished, and God is pleased.

Jesus was a virgin.

Do you have a problem with that?

------ # & ! $ # + % ----

CLICK IT: www.FourLetterWords.org/wait

SCAN IT:

Theologically, this country is at present in a state of utter chaos, established in the name of religious toleration, and rapidly degenerating into the flight from reason and the death of hope. We are not happy in this condition, and there are signs of a very great eagerness, especially among the younger people, to find a creed to which they can give wholehearted adherence. This is the church's opportunity, if she chooses to take it.[1]

Dorothy Sayers, England, 1940's

------ # & ! $ # + % ----

Touchy Ideas

1. I know I'm going to heaven because I belong to Jesus.
2. I have God in my life, through Christ alone.
3. Life is tough, but life is good. I have hope.
4. I'm certain of it.

Touchy Ideas

1. But these are written that you may believe that Jesus is the Christ, the Son of God, and that believing you may have life in His name. (John 20:31)
2. These things I have written to you who believe in the name of the Son of God, that you may know that you have eternal life, and that you may continue to believe in the name of the Son of God. (1 John 5:13)
3. I do not pray for these alone, but also for those who will believe in Me through their word. (John 17:20)

------ # & ! $ # + % ----

THE SQUID PUSHED ME over the edge. Or, I should say, to the edge. Other than my dad, I was the last man standing. My brother, Bob, and my friends, Karl and Sherri, had already heaved their guts into the cruel sea, and scurried like little cowards to the bunks below decks.

I, however, kept my lunch down and braved the waves topside with my dad on a three-hour tour. A dozen other passengers had also dropped like flies. Only a handful of intrepid landlubbers remained to probe the choppy Gulf of Mexico for angler bragging rights.

I never did get my hand on a fishing pole.

An iron fist gripped my stomach and squeezed harder with each rising swell. The ship's captain promised calmer waters ahead, and chugged toward it. I prayed a passionate boyhood prayer: *God, don't let me puke.*

A queasy feeling stretched from my throat to belly. Even my cheeks felt funny. My nose rebelled as the salt air blended with the omnipresent aroma of decayed fish and everybody's vomit.

I sat next to my dad on a bench. He smiled, smoked a pipe, and enjoyed the sunny day.

"Dad, don't you feel funny inside?" My nine-year old voice quavered a bit.

"No, son. I got used to it in the military."

"Oh..."

About that time, a sadistic deck hand brought out the bait.

Trays of chopped, raw squid.

That's how the squid pushed me to the edge. I now understand the purpose of the handrail that runs the circumference of a ship. The deck hand laughed at me. He'd grown accustomed to the motion of the sea.

The next two hours saw me alternately writhing in agony on a bunk beside my brother and friends, and chumming the warm Gulf waters.

To add to the insult, when at long last we stepped onto beautiful Mother Earth, the ground beneath my feet continued to rise and fall. It took a full hour to get over that particular gift from the sea.

What mattered was that I was ashore. Hallelujah. I felt like kissing the ground.

Modern society has lived so long on uncertainty and skepticism we've become used to it. Like the ship's deckhand, the instability feels normal to us.

Like weightlessness feels normal to an astronaut.

But astronauts were not designed for weightlessness.

And we were not designed for truthlessness.

It's hard to feel secure when life's basic truths are up for grabs—including whether or not there is truth. Or whether or not you actually exist. We are already reaping the fruits of society's cynicism against truth: anxiety, irrationality, and despair.

God set his church on the edge of the turbulent sea, high on an immoveable rock, to be a lighthouse guiding "whosoever wills" to Jesus Christ.

Because nobody was designed for a truth that won't stay true.

Or a God who won't stay God.

People crave the solid rock, Jesus. They just don't know it yet.

Dorothy Sayers's exhortation to her generation nails it for ours. There are "signs of a very great eagerness, especially among the younger people, to find a creed to which they can give wholehearted adherence."

Finding My Creed

I found my creed in a high school gym. In the spring of my junior year, I was sitting in the bleachers of Chicago's Lane Technical High School, reading a book about God and the devil.

My gym coach was absent. On those days we used the hour as a study hall. I used it to chase down answers to my spiritual frustrations.

The last part of the book described the devil's tactic to manipulate Christ's followers through *guilt*. The author compared guilt to a handle attached to my back. He explained how Satan grabbed the handle, slammed me around and sent me crawling back to my half-hearted life.

I sat, mesmerized, on hard wooden bleachers. My heart pounded and my palms grew sweaty.

I was on the verge of something, but didn't know of what.

Until the topic switched from my guilt to Christ's cross. I found the first explanation of the death of Jesus that ever made sense for me. I had heard the story a million times. But this was the first time it clicked.

The Cross of Christ became my solid rock. I took my stand, and have been standing there ever since.

Christ, crucified and living again, is my creed.

At the Cross, Jesus crushed the head of evil, conquering Satan and his despicable minions.

At the Cross, Jesus absorbed the sin of the world: everybody's sins, including mine.

At the Cross, Jesus took the hit I deserved. He endured not only my sin, but also the holy wrath of God against my sin, and drowned them both in the depths of his sacrifice.

At the Cross, Jesus battered down the gates of hell and unlocked the gates of heaven for all who would opt in to his amazing grace.

At the Cross, Jesus bequeathed his last will and testament: my inheritance, a portfolio of assets that provides absolutely perfect resources for every circumstance of this life, and for every promised pleasure of the next.

At the Cross, Jesus anchored my heart to God's.

The death of Christ was the death of death, including the mini-death we experience every day trying to build a life while far from God. Jesus brought me near to God, here and now. He moved into me, indwelling me with his Spirit. He gave me a new name, a new identity, a new nature, a new purpose, a new community, and a new hope.

By means of the Cross, God served up a new vocabulary of four letter words: holy, gift, love, hope, and *joie* (it's French, but it's four letters). He made sense of all the other four letter words, like the box top makes sense of jumbled puzzle pieces. I'm not saying I've put all the pieces together yet. But I'm at peace, knowing one day, the puzzle will be complete.

My Jesus creed presses all the right buttons inside me. I want to live for him. Nobody has to force me. I want to tell the world about him. I want to go deeper into him, to fathom the depths of his love and the heights of his holiness.

I want to.

His story stirs up wholehearted allegiance within me.

Naturally.

Hope for This World

No force on earth has given the world as much hope as Jesus. From day one, he launched his followers on a worldwide mission to alleviate human suffering. The crucifixion, the mother lode of human despair, became the Cross, the world's enduring symbol of hope. By heroic deeds of courage and self-sacrifice, Christ's followers turned a dark world upside down. They did this as a *response* to Christ's work on the cross.

Subtract Christianity's influence, and the world slinks back to the yesteryear's theater of cruelty.

What have Christians given to society? Here's a partial list.

- The Church is the largest single supplier of healthcare and education on the planet. This applies especially to blackspots often forgotten by the rest of the world. Most of this is supplied without profit.[3]

- Christians pioneered social work, going back to the days of Constantine. It was Christ's followers who first established "poor houses, homes for the aged, orphanages, and hospitals."[4]

- In the modern era, Jane Adams, motivated by faith in Christ, took up that work, founding America's first "settlement house," seeking to bridge the chasm between rich and poor. For this, she was the first American woman awarded the Nobel Peace Prize.[5]

- A Christian minister, Rev. Benjamin Waugh, became the driving force behind London's Society for the Prevention of Cruelty to Children in the late 1880's. This society altered the perception of children and helped institute child labor laws in the western world.[6]

- Save the Children, a worldwide relief organization, also started by Christians, was largely responsible when the League of Nations (forerunner of the United Nations) adopted the Declaration of the Rights of the Child.[7]

- Bernardo's Homes, the world's largest orphanage system, was founded by Thomas John Bernardo, an evangelical Christian.[8]

- A dedicated Christian, Josephine Butler, became an early advocate for the welfare of prostitutes. She campaigned for America's first laws establishing an age of consent for sexual activity with a minor.[9]

- William Wilberforce, converted to Christ in 1785, led the charge to abolish slavery in the Western world, as beautifully depicted in the film, *Amazing Grace*.[10]

- Christ's followers led the way in care for the elderly and disabled. Christians instituted the world's first "alms-houses" even before the 1100's. These were the forerunners of today's rescue missions.[11]

- The Quakers, a pacifist Christian group, brought about prison reform during the Victorian Era. They fought to ensure humane conditions and lobbied for education and therapy for prisoners in the U.K. and the U.S.[12]

- Louis Braille designed the system of raised dots to offer the gift of reading to the blind. He extended his creation to music as well as words, opening worlds previously closed to his sight-challenged friends.[13]

- Rev. Thomas Hopkins Gallaudet pioneered education for the deaf and raised money to open North America's first educational institution for the deaf.[14]

- In 1911, Douglas MacMillan established the Society for the Prevention and Relief of Cancer, the first institution of its kind. It continues today as one of Britain's largest charities, and has birthed similar organizations around the world.[15]

- Millard Fuller, a successful lawyer and businessman as well as a committed follower of Jesus, launched a ministry called Koinonia House. *Koinonia* is the biblical word for community or fellowship. Fuller built homes for those unable to afford them. He then built Koinonia House into the global agency now called Habitat for Humanity.[16]

- The Salvation Army, caring for the poor and downtrodden around the world, was started by William and Katherine Booth, evangelical ministers. Wanting to preach the gospel, they fed people first because they believed, "Hungry bellies have no ears."[17]

- Mother Teresa won a Nobel Peace Prize for founding the Missionaries of Charity, embracing India's untouchables. At her death, the order provided "610 missions in 123 countries, including hospices and homes for people with HIV/AIDS, leprosy and tuberculosis, soup kitchens, children's and family counselling programs, orphanages, and schools."[18]

- In both the U.K. and U.S., the first free schools were established by churches to teach illiterate street children to read. Public education was an outgrowth of these "ragged schools."[19]

Christians were the first to fight cruelty against animals, led the way in the education of women, have done more to promote global literacy than any other group, are the first to serve destitute children and adults in poverty stricken areas of the word, are leaders in the struggle to heal and prevent AIDS, invented microfinance for third world enterprises, and founded life-changing organizations like Alcoholics Anonymous, Amnesty International, and Oxfam (a pioneer in famine relief).

An amazing record for the flawed followers of the perfect Son of God.[20]

Hope for the world. Not just in heaven, but on earth too.

If you value freedom, education, health, literacy, stewardship of earth, and care for the marginalized, you owe a debt of gratitude to Christians.

Jesus compared his band of followers to salt in the earth. Take away the salt, he said, and you take away the preservative. A world

powered by BWSCAN.com
CHRISTIAN GOOD IN THE WORLD

without Christians would be... well, would be just as harsh as the many places in the world today without a Christian heritage.

Here's my point: if you want a force for good in the world, a force that draws forth whatever beauty lies dormant in the human heart, and if you want a force that makes sense logically, philosophically, relationally, psychologically, theologically, and aesthetically, there is no serious contender beside the historic, biblical Christian faith.

The Jesus Creed.

You are invited to follow the One who healed lepers, embraced sinners, and instructed his followers to give a cup of cold water every time a neighbor's throat felt parched. He wasn't content to leave four letter words like Ouch, and Evil just hanging there, festering, driving a wedge between people and people or between people and God.

He didn't just preach of a better life after this one—though he did that—he also worked for a better life here and now.

The evidence suggests his followers got the message.

Strength for today.

Bright hope for tomorrow.

Confidence in a beautiful heaven forever.

That's what Christians offer the world.

Hope for the World to Come

If the Jesus way is the true way to God, or if it's the only way—if it's the one and only trail from this life to the next—shouldn't we tell the world? Shouldn't we evangelize? If we care about our friends, shouldn't we gently pester them to at least investigate the treasure we have found in Jesus?

This treasure is described in breathtaking detail in Scripture. The truths of Scripture are not disconnected bits of random advice floating through the cosmos. They are a single, interlocking system, like Legos. Every truth fits with every other truth. They connect. Together, they create a beautiful masterpiece: a revelation of the heart of God.

Scripture is coherent because every line flows from the heart of a God who matches the deep needs of the human heart.

In God's heart, we discover a quality absent from every other god, every other philosophy, and every other religion in world history.

We discover *grace*. We discover God's amazing readiness to reach down to us, and to do for us what we cannot do for ourselves. Grace honors God's love without dishonoring God's holiness. Grace is love made righteous; it is love for unholy people legitimized without creating legal fiction.

Grace makes God "just and the justifier of the one who has faith in Jesus" (Romans 3:26). *Just* in this verse means righteous and consistent with his own standards of perfection. *Justifier* means God declares us to be righteous and consistent with his standards because we've put our faith in Christ. God declares unrighteous train wrecks, like me and you, to be righteous in his sight.

How?

By means of the Cross.

This is grace. Not leniency. Not bland niceness. Not God overlooking our faults. But God facing them squarely, seeing our truth, rolling up his sleeves, and plunging into our dirt, all the way to death. God reached down because he knew we could never reach up even if we wanted to.

Grace.

The Bible's God owns it.

It's the only system that makes sense.

Grace is the exclusive treasure of the Christian faith. It births hope. It's the pot of gold at the end of the seeker's rainbow.

I've been walking this trail for almost fifty years. I've been pointing people to it since elementary school. I confess I haven't always lived up to my creed. I have let Jesus down and I've let my friends down.

But God has never let me down.

And I've never met a person who wasn't happy when they came to Christ.

Beaming.

Relieved.

Changed.

Hopeful.

I'm a preacher, and as often as I preach this message, I see men and women cross the line of faith. I see giant smiles. Tears of joy. I see couples and families take the plunge together. I see lives changed, and brokenness healed.

I've seen it. It's real. I've felt it myself. That's the power of love. That's amazing grace. That's Jesus.

Some things are true and some things are false.

You will never find a truth as true as Jesus.

He is so true that, by contrast, every competing claim is false.

Try him.

See for yourself.

------ # & ! $ # + % ----

Talking Points

I'm changing the focus of this final Talking Points section of *Four Letter Words.* In this conversation, don't picture yourself talking to a friend from school or work, picture yourself talking to God. Picture yourself moving close to him, like a toddler pressing against a good Daddy. Here is a sample prayer you can echo to God if you have never before crossed the line of faith. If you've never made it official. It's spiritual dynamite. Use it if you mean it.

1. Admit.

Dear God, I admit I need you. I've been far from you, like the prodigal son. I've gone my own way, and it isn't working. I've thrown a thousand arguments your way. Most of them were honest questions, but I admit some of them were just plain stubbornness. I need you. I admit I can't find you on my own. I admit I have sinned. I haven't lived up to your standards. I haven't even lived up to my own standards. I admit it, God.

2. Believe.

I believe that Jesus Christ is my way to you. I believe he is your Son. I believe he died on the cross for my sins. I believe he rose again.

I don't know how it all works, but I'm telling you, God, I believe in Jesus. What he did by dying and rising again opened the way to you. What he did made it right for you to forgive me, love me, adopt me, and commune with me. Jesus did that. Not me. Not my religion. Not my good deeds. Just Jesus. As best as I can, I'm telling you, God, I'm believing in Jesus.

3. Choose.

Right now I choose to trust him as my *only* hope. Right now I choose to embrace him. I declare Jesus as my Savior. I choose to step across the line of faith. I open my life and heart to Jesus. I officially renounce all other confidences, and lean all my weight on Jesus. I'm not leaning on my good deeds, or religion, or rituals. Just Jesus. He is my hope. His death and resurrection made it possible for me to connect with you, God. His death and resurrection made it possible for me to have the life I've always dreamed of—a life with you, God, at the core. Thank you for reaching down to me through Jesus. Thank you for the gift of eternal life in him. Thank you for coming to live inside me. I don't know what that's going to do to me, but I'm ready. I'm asking you, God, right now, for Jesus' sake, please save me.

When you speak to God like this, he hears. He always answers. He's never rejected anyone yet. He won't reject you. Instead, he'll bring you close to himself, and make your life brand new.

Your next steps are super important. Scan this QR code to visit www.startingwithgod.com, a ministry of Campus Crusade for Christ. You'll find a boatload of resources: a church locator, relevant articles, and a free subscription to ongoing spiritual guidance through email. Think of it as your personal online Gandalf to guide your next steps.

powered by BWSCAN.com

STARTING
WITH GOD

Get into a great church. Shop around till you find one that fits. Partner with a campus group or youth group that loves God, loves the Bible, and loves you. Your spiritual journey is yours, but it shouldn't be yours alone. Read the Gospel of John in the Bible. Underline every time you see the word "faith" or "believe."

I'm excited for you and your unfolding story ahead.

Welcome to the best four letter word of all: welcome to God's infinite, matchless, blood-bought, unfailing boundless, perfect, glorious *LOVE*.

------ # & ! $ # + % ----

CLICK IT: www.FourLetterWords.org/hope

SCAN IT:

powered by BWSCAN.com

DISCUSSION GUIDE

Download a printable discussion guide with additional space for writing and journalling at www.FourLetterWords.org.

Chapter 1

1. How do most of your friends feel about most Christians? About Christianity? What do you feel about most Christians?
2. Talk about a time when your faith got you into trouble. How did you respond? Would you do something differently next time?
3. Has a professor, teacher, or mentor ever criticized your faith? What was the specific criticism?
4. Read Acts 17:16-34. How did Paul forge a connection with the religious pluralists on Mars' Hill?

Chapter 2: TRUE

1. Has anyone ever told you, "Just because it's true for you doesn't make it true for me?" How did you respond? Have you ever told somebody that?
2. What do you think of Avicenna's argument for the Principle of Non-contradiction?
3. Are your friends at work or on campus more likely to believe truth is relative or absolute? How have you heard this expressed?
4. Where would you place your own view of truth on the spectrum between modernism and post-modernism? Are there any truths true for all people of all places and all times? Can you name a few?
5. What does Romans 3:4 say about God, humans, and truth?

Chapter 3: KNOW

1. Can we know anything for sure?
2. Describe a conversation in which faith was treated like a flaw in the system. Have you ever felt stumped by the critique that you

rely on faith but your friends rely on science or logic? How did you respond?

3. How do you know most of what you know? If faith is confidence in an authority, name a few authorities you have placed your confidence in.

4. What role does the Bible play in helping you know what you know?

5. What does Jude 3 say about the earliest followers of Jesus and how certain they were of what they knew?

Chapter 4: PAIN

1. How has the pain in your life affected your view of God? Do you hold any bitterness in your heart against God? How does that show itself in your relationship with him?

2. How have you heard friends or family express the problem of pain? In your experience, how big is this problem? Have you ever heard someone state some version of the Inconsistent Triad?

3. Can a committed naturalist worry about the problem of pain without being inconsistent? Why or why not?

4. What does 2 Corinthians 1:2,3 say about God's heart when we suffer?

Chapter 5: OUCH

1. How has the "all is one" viewpoint been expressed by your friends or family? What does this view say about good and evil?

2. What does Christ's death on the cross suggest about God's understanding of human pain? How well do you think God understands your own struggles and pain?

3. If you could send God one message about your suffering, what would you want him to know?

4. How do you feel when God doesn't answer your prayer? What do you say to friends when God doesn't answer their prayers?

5. How does setting your pain in "an eternal context" change things?

6. What do you feel and think about Hebrews 2:18?

Chapter 6: EVIL

1. What would most of your friends say about the statement that "evil is just a point of view?"
2. Do good and evil truly balance out or does good win in the end?
3. Respond to Francis Schaeffer's quote on pp. 103, 104. In your opinion, how does today's cultural turmoil relate to the teachings of moral relativism and naturalism?
4. How does the death of Jesus deliver the ultimate blow to cosmic evil? What would be different if Christ had not died?
5. What does 1 Corinthians 15:24-26 imply about Jesus' ultimate victory over evil?

Chapter 7: WORD

1. What comes to mind when you hear that God is love? Deep inside, do you feel that God is love?
2. How does the biblical claim that God is love compare with the teachings of other major religions? In your opinion, in what ways does God's love set the Bible in a class by itself?
3. What view of Scriptures did Jesus hold? How well does your view match his view?
4. Does any other sacred book offer the world the kind of love Jesus displayed on Calvary's cross?
5. What does Jesus imply about Scripture in John 14:23,24?

Chapter 8: DAMN

1. How has the idea of hell influenced your view of Christianity and God? Your friends' view?
2. Which of the five views of hell seems most biblical? Which do you think is least biblical?
3. Has your belief in hell ever impacted one of your relationships? How? What conversations on this topic have made a difference in your life? What would you say differently?
4. What comes to mind when you think about the holiness and justice of God? Can God be God and not be holy?

5. What does Jesus' death on the cross say about the holiness and love of God?

6. How does 2 Peter 3:9 inform your view of hell?

Chapter 9: WAIT

1. What do your friends think about the Bible's teachings on sex? How relevant for today are these teachings, in your opinion? In your friends' opinions?

2. Have you ever been viewed as weird or judgmental because of your sexual obedience to Jesus? Have you been accused of being narrow, rigid, or arrogant?

3. How would you summarize the Bible's teaching on sexual activity?

4. What changes would you have to make to bring yourself in line with these teachings? Are you willing to make those changes? Do you need a support network to make them?

5. How can you help yourself or your friends follow God's will for their sexuality?

6. What sexual guidance is offered in 1 Corinthians 6:18?

Chapter 10: HOPE

1. Respond to Dorothy Sayers's statement at the beginning of the chapter. How much does her statement apply to today?

2. How much uncertainty about truth swirls around your friends and coworkers?

3. What do you feel and think when you read the list of Christian good in the world? How does this list match up with your perceptions about Christianity? Your friends' perceptions?

4. Which items on the list are most important to you and why?

5. In what ways can you and your group get involved in bringing hope to the world?

6. What does John 3:16 say about the way God expressed his love for the world? What is keeping you from stepping across the line of faith right now?

NOTES

2-True

1. "Portrait of Socrates" in marble. Photo by Eric Gaba. Used by permission. This file is licensed under the Creative Commons Attribution ShareAlike 2.5 License. In short: you are free to share and make derivative works of the file under the conditions that you appropriately attribute it, and that you distribute it only under a license identical to this one. All photos herein attributed to the Creative Commons share this permission.

2. Picture of Avicenna the Physician. Used by permission. Copyright © The Circle of Ancient Iranian Studies (CAIS) Permission is granted to copy, distribute and/or modify this document under the terms of the GNU Free Documentation License, Version 1.2 or any later version published by the Free Software Foundation; with no Invariant Sections, no Front-Cover Texts, and no Back-Cover Texts. All photos herein attributed to the GNU Free Documentation License share this permission.

3. Avicenna, an Islamic philosopher, writing around eight centuries after Christ. In *Metaphysics, I*; commenting on Aristotle, Topics I.11.105a4–5, cited from Wikipedia, "Law of non-contradiction."

4. Google "William Wilberforce" or watch the movie *Amazing Grace*.

5. Jesus put flesh on his counter-cultural opinion that women and men were equal in places like John 4:4-27 (the woman at the well, see esp. v. 47) and John 8:1-11 (the woman taken in adultery, where the guilty man was missing and where he called her "woman" used as an ennobling term).

6. Carl Sagan. *The Cosmos* (Ballantine Books, 1985), p. 1.

7. Ravi Zacharias, "Address to the United Nations Prayer Breakfast," at http://www.rzim.org/GlobalElements/GFV/tabid/449/ArticleID/96/CBModuleId/1045/Default.aspx?id=13

8. Tozer in *God Tells the Man Who Cares,* (Harrisburg, PA: Christian Publications, Inc.,1970), pp. 3,4.

9. Nietzsche, *The Will to Power* (trans. Walter Kaufmann and R. Hollingdale, New York: Random House, 1968), p. 267.

10. "They do blaspheme who say: Allah is one of three in a Trinity, for there is no god except One Allah" (Qur'an 5:73). To blaspheme is to insult God and all that is sacred.

3-Know

1. Proslogion, ch. 2; Gregory Schufreider. *Confessions of a Rational Mystic: Anselm's Early Writings* (West Lafayette, Ind.: Purdue University Press, 1994) pp. 324-5.

2. Friedrich Nietzsche, *Sämtliche Werke: Kritische Studienausgabe, vol. 5,* p. 96, eds. Giorgio Colli and Mazzino Montinari, Berlin, de Gruyter (1980). Beyond Good and Evil, "Fourth Part: Maxims and Interludes," section 134 (1886).

3. Georg Wilhelm Friedrich Hegel (1770–1831). *Philosophy of Right,* preface, p. 10, Oxford University Press (1952).

4. Paul Davies, "Taking Science on Faith." In *The New York Times,* November 24, 2007. It's worth the read, at http://www.nytimes.com/2007/11/24/opinion/24davies.html?pagewanted=1&_r=1

5. "Axiom" at www.Wikipedia.org. September, 2008.

6. See the amazing interview of Dr. Francis S. Collins by Ian Miller in SFGate.com

at http://articles.sfgate.com/2006-08-07/news/17305535_1_dr-francis-s-collins-human-genome-project-atheist.

4-Pain

1. Picture of Epicurus, public domain. Used by permission, from http://en.wikipedia. org/wiki/Image:Epicurus_bust2.jpg.
2. Quote from Epicurus cited in Brad Inwood and Lloyd P. Gerson, *Hellenistic Philosophy: Introductory Readings*. Hackett Publishing, 1997. Page 94.
3. Ibid.
4. Quoted in Rick Rood, "The Problem of Evil: How could a good God allow evil?" at LeadershipU, http://www.leaderu.com/orgs/probe/docs/evil.html.
5. Theodicy. (n.d.). *Webster's Revised Unabridged Dictionary.* Retrieved September 20, 2008, from Dictionary.com website: http://dictionary.reference.com/browse/theodicy
6. http://en.wikipedia.org/wiki/Biosphere_2
7. Picture of Thales of Miletus, in the public domain according to: http://en.wikipedia. org/wiki/Image:Thales.jpg
8. *The Blind Watchmaker* (London and New York: W.W. Norton & Co., 1986) p. 5.
9. Margaret Y. MacDonald, Daniel J. Harrington, Donald P. Senior. *Colossians and Ephesians.* Liturgical Press, 2000. Page. 61, note on v. 17.
10. Photo of Christ Pantocrator mosaic and St Catherine's Church. This file is licensed under the Creative Commons Attribution-Share Alike 3.0 Unported license.

5-Ouch

1. Mikhail Gorbachev quoted on www.pantheism.net, retrieved March 13, 2011.
2. "Colors of the Wind," lyrics by Steven Schwartz, 1995.
3. Pocahontas was the first known convert to Christianity among Native Americans. Public Domain: http://www.lib.utexas.edu/photodraw/portraits/ Original: Clarke, Mary Cowden (1883). World Noted Women. New York: D. Appleton and Company.
4. From the Eric Butterworth website, September 23, 2008, at: http://ericbutterworth. com/html/about.html
5. Francis Schaeffer, *He Is There and He Is Not Silent* (Wheaton: Tyndale), 1972, beginning at p. 9 and throughout.
6. Quoted in Peter Jones, *Pagans in the Pews* (Regal Books, 2001), p. 33.
7. In the article "Heroic Virtue," *Gnosis*, Summer 1992, pp. 36-42 or online at http:// www.gratefulness.org/readings/dsr_HeroicVirtue5.htm, retrieved June 19, 2011.
8. From the Hsin-Hsin Ming, quoted in Donald S. Lopez, *A Modern Buddhist Bible* (Beacon Press, 2002), p. 166.
9. Samyutta Nikaya 56,11.
10. Photo of the Buddha in the Public Domain, from http://en.wikipedia.org/wiki/Image: Gandhara_Buddha_(tnm).jpeg.
11. Hebrews 9:12,26; 1 Peter 1:20; 1 Timothy 2:5.
12. Oprah says, "And you know, it's been a journey to get to the place where I understand, that what I believe is that Jesus came to show us Christ consciousness. That Jesus came to show us the way of the heart and that what Jesus was saying that to show us the higher consciousness that we're all talking about here." Quoted in Steve Cable, "Oprah's Spirituality: Exploring 'A New Earth'" on Probe Ministry's website, at http:// www.probe.org/site/c.fdKEIMNsEoG/b.4217681/ on October 2, 2008.
13. C.S. Lewis. *The Problem of Pain.* London: Geoffrey Bles: The Centenary Press, 1940. p. 28.
14. Hebrews 12:29; Isaiah 6:3; 1 John 4:8,16.

15. Lewis, ibid.
16. Art in public Domain. Gustave Dore. "Satan Encounters Death and Sin," from Paradise Lost, illustration 8.

6-Evil

1. Quoted in Varla Ventura, T*he Book of the Bizarre: Freaky Facts and Strange Stories,* Weiser, 2008. Page 260.
2. Artwork entitled: Jan Hus at the Stake. This is a faithful photographic reproduction of an original two-dimensional work of art. The work of art itself is in the public domain for the following reason: This image (or other media file) is in the public domain because its copyright has expired. This applies to the United States, Canada, the European Union and those countries with a copyright term of life of the author plus 70 years.
3. Wikipedia. "Jan Hus." http://en.wikipedia.org/wiki/Jan_Hus
4. C. S. Lewis. *Mere Christianity,* p. 15.
5. Norman Geisler. Can Atheists Justify Being Good Without God? at http://www.normangeisler.net/atheismbegood.html, March 23, 2009.
6. The Barna Group, The Barna Update, "Americans Are More Likely to Base Truth on Feelings."
7. Wikipedia. "Moral Absolutism," March 29, 2009.
8. C.S. Lewis, quoted in Peter Kreeft, *C.S. Lewis for the third millennium: six essays on the abolition of man* (Ignatius Press, 1994), p. 112.
9. Cited in Louis P. Pojman, *Moral Philosophy: A Reader* (Hackett Publishing, 2003), third edition. In Pojman, "A Defense of Ethical Objectivism," p. 38.
10. Walter C. Kaiser, Peter H. Davids, Frederick Fyvie Bruce, Manfred T. Brauch. *Hard Sayings of the Bible* (InterVarsity Press, 1996), p. 357.
11. Francis Schaeffer. *A Christian View of Philophy and Culture* (Crossway Books, 1985), p. 232.
12. Interview with Cindy Crosby, "Interview with a Penitent" in *Christianity Today,* posted online December 1, 2005, at http://www.christianitytoday.com/ct/2005/december/11.50.html?start=1.

7-Word

1. Source unknown. This quote is commonly attributed to Mark Twain, though I have been unable to find its source. Whether or not Twain wrote it, it perfectly captures an honest person's reaction.
2. Tan Swee Eng, "A Basic Buddhism Guide." Buddhanet.net (2004), cited in "Is Buddhism Atheistic?" at http://www.religionfacts.com/buddhism/beliefs/atheism.htm on April 29, 2009.
3. al-Faruqi, *Christian Mission and Islamic Da`wah: Proceedings of the Chambèsy Dialogue Consultation* (Leicester: The Islamic Foundation, 1982), 47-48, cited in "Muslim Beliefs About God" at http://www.religionfacts.com/islam/beliefs/god.htm#2 on April 30, 2009.
4. From The Hindu Universe website, at www.Hindunet.com.
5. "The Jefferson Bible" on Wikipedia.
6. R.J. Rummel, "How Many did Communist Regimes Murder?" at http://www.hawaii.edu/powerkills/COM.ART.HTM.
7. From the Wiccan Spirituality website: http://www.wicca-spirituality.com/wiccan-goddesses.html retrieved June 20, 2011.
8. Picture of Ra, the Egyptian Sun God, used by permission. This file is licensed under the

Creative Commons Attribution-Share Alike 3.0 Unported, 2.5 Generic, 2.0 Generic and 1.0 Generic license.

9. Picture of the Prodigal Son: Published before 1923 and in the public domain in the U.S. This file is licensed under the Creative Commons Attribution-Share Alike 3.0 Unported, 2.5 Generic, 2.0 Generic and 1.0 Generic license.

10. http://www.al-islam.org/greater_sins_complete/28.htm, see paragraph 6.

11. http://kaladarshan.arts.ohio-state.edu/resources/downloads/sutras/01earlyTexts/ Karma%20sutra.pdf "To vituperate (abuse) your parents will cause you to be reborn a deaf mute in your next incarnation."

12. http://en.wikipedia.org/wiki/Karma_in_Hinduism. The prodigal's bad deeds would be added to the weight of negative karma to be paid out in this and future lifetimes.

8-Damn

1. *The Knowledge of the Holy,* 1975, p. 95.

2. De Spectaculis, Chapter XXX.

3. From his sermon, "The Eternity of Hell Torments."

4. Quoted in Hypatia Bradlaugh Bonner, *The Christian Hell: From the First to the Twentieth Century* (1913?), p. 38.

5. In Nancy Haught, "Ten Minutes with the UCC's Carlton Pearson" on the United Church of Christ website, retrieved August 13, 2009.

6. The term "Anonymous Christians," was coined by Catholic theologian, Karl Rahner. For a discussion, see LeRoy Miller and Stanley James Grenz, eds., *Fortress Introduction To Contemporary Theologies* (Augsburg Fortress Publishers, 1998), pp. 194, ff.

7. From Walter M. Abbott, *The Documents of Vatican II* (New York: Guild Press, 1966), 35, as cited by K. Neill Foster in "Implicit Christians: An Evangelical Appraisal" in Alliance Academic Review.com, retrieved on July 29, 2009, http://www.allianceacademicreview.com/1998/AAR1998-7Foster.php

8. "I'm a Universalist who believes in Hell... [Grace] is ours simply because God has invited us to the party. We're in unless we choose to be out. That is how grace works. We don't opt in to it – we can only opt out." Spencer Burke, *A Heretic's Guide to Eternity* (John Wiley and Sons, 2006), pp. 196, 202.

9. Brian McLaren describes a conversation with his daughter, Jess: "I tried to help Jess that Saturday afternoon by telling her about "inclusivism," an alternative to the "exclusivist" view she was unhappy with. While exclusivism limited eternal life in heaven to bona fide, confessing Christians, inclusivism kept the door open that others could be saved through Christ even if they never identified as Christians... Exclusivism was my starting point, inclusivism was my fall-back, and conditionalism [that Hell and/or its punishment is temporary] was my last resort." In his article on Beliefnet.com, "If Christianity Is True, People I Love Will Burn in Hell," retrieved July 30, 2009. McLaren has not yet self-identified with any specific position on universalism other than to say he is not a universalist, though his writings flirt with and tend toward universalism.

10. "New-school believers are asking if it is possible for people who do not know the true Jesus to still be covered by his redemptive work, because he (alone) knows their hearts." Without explicitly affirming universalism, the authors hint at it strongly in this chapter. Chuck Smith Jr. (not to be confused with his father, the founder of the Calvary Chapel movement) and Matt Whitlock, *Frequently Avoided Questions* (Baker Books, 2005), p. 166.

11. Joseph Tkach, President of Grace Communion International, formerly known as the Worldwide Church of God. The quote is from "Is Jesus the Only Way?" article on the church's website, http://www.wcg.org/lit/gospel/oneway.htm, retrieved July 31, 2009.

12. Rob Bell, *Love Wins* (Harper Collins, 2011), p. 105.
13. "God discerns who among the heathen truly searches for the Good" and offers them salvation after death. Clark H. Pinnock, "Why Is Jesus the Only Way?" *Eternity*, December, 1976, 15.
14. 1 Corinthians 15:18,20,51; 1 Thessalonians 4:14-16.
15. Technically, there is a difference. *Conditional immortality* teaches that humans are not immortal until they receive Jesus. *Annihilationism* teaches that humans are born immortal, but lose their immortality when they die without Jesus. The final effect is identical: existence-less-ness.
16. David L. Edwards and John Stott. *Evangelical Essentials: A Liberal-Evangelical Dialogue* (Hodder and Stoughton, 1988), pp. 314,5.
17. There is a huge variety with Adventism, so ask first. The Seventh Day Adventist online teaching ministry, *The Biblical Research Institute*, states, "Those who die are naked in the biblical sense of being dispossessed of everything, even of their existence." From the article, "From Life to Life" on the BRI website, retrieved August 3, 2009.
18. Quoted in Richard Dawkins, *The God Delusion*. (Houghton Mifflin Company, 2006) p. 279.
19. First Apology, 52.
20. Apology 18:3
21. Michael Green. *Evangelism in the Early Church* (William B. Eerdmans Publishing Co, 2004) p. 249.
22. "Gehenna" in William Smith. *Dictionary of the Bible,* 1868. "The conception of the writer appears to have been, that at the time of the Messianic judgment the wicked would be gathered in the Valley of Hinnom in the presence of the righteous, where the earth would open, as in the case of the followers of Korah (Nu 16:30), and receive them into the fiery lake beneath. From this conception of "the accursed valley" as the gate of hell, the transfer of the name Gehenna to the place of punishment itself (comp. the Latin Avernus) was easy and natural."
23. Exodus 23:24; Ezekiel 34:13,14; 2 Chronicles 34:3-7; Acts 15:29; 17:16; 1 Corinthians 8:4; 2 Corinthians 6:16.
24. Hear Todd Adams's message on .mp3 by scanning the QR code or going here: http://bit.ly/lrtrly.
25. John Hannah, quoted at http://hungryforgodsword.blogspot.com/2009/03/reality-of-hell.html
26. Quoted in Lieghton Ford, *Good News is for Sharing* (David C. Cook Publishing Co., 1877), p. 34.
27. Michael Green. Evangelism in the Early Church, p. 249.

9-Wait

1. John Piper. *The Other Dark Exchange: Homosexuality,* Part 1, October 11, 1998, www.DesiringGod.org, Used by Permission.
2. The image is from Albrecht Durer, 1504. Public domain. http://www.backtoclassics.com/gallery/albrechtdurer/adam_and_eve3/
3. *The Bible Knowledge Commentary* in comment on Gal. 5:19.
4. Vito Rispo. "Understanding the Human Herd Mentality" in AdSavvy. At http://www.adsavvy.org/understanding-the-human-herd-mentality/, retrieved3/6/2011.
5. Sharon Jayson. "Sooner vs. Later: Is there ideal age for first marriage?" in USAToday 11/9/08, retrieved 3/7/11 from http://www.usatoday.com/news/health/2008-11-09-delayed-marriage_N.htm.
6. Ibid.

7.   Image of Telemachus and Mentor by Pablo E. Fabisch 1699, public domain.

10-Hope

1.   Dorothy Sayers in *Creed or Chaos* (Sophia Institute Press, 1995), p. 45.
2.   Gustave Doré. "The Darkness of the Crucifixion." Art in public domain.
3.   http://entertainment.timesonline.co.uk/tol/arts_and_entertainment/the_tls/article6057334.ece
4.   http://en.wikipedia.org/wiki/History_of_social_work
5.   http://en.wikipedia.org/wiki/Jane_Addams
6.   http://en.wikipedia.org/wiki/National_Society_for_the_Prevention_of_Cruelty_to_Children#History
7.   http://en.wikipedia.org/wiki/Eglantyne_Jebb
8.   http://en.wikipedia.org/wiki/Thomas_John_Barnardo
9.   http://en.wikipedia.org/wiki/Josephine_Butler
10. http://en.wikipedia.org/wiki/William_Wilberforce
11. http://en.wikipedia.org/wiki/Almshouse
12. http://en.wikipedia.org/wiki/Prison_reform#United_Kingdom
13. http://74.84.206.112/ChurchHistory/11630360/
14. http://en.wikipedia.org/wiki/Thomas_Hopkins_Gallaudet
15. http://en.wikipedia.org/wiki/Douglas_Macmillan
16. http://en.wikipedia.org/wiki/Millard_Fuller
17. http://en.wikipedia.org/wiki/William_Booth
18. http://en.wikipedia.org/wiki/Mother_Teresa
19. http://en.wikipedia.org/wiki/John_Pounds
20. Credit for this entire roster of Christian good goes to: http://christiangoodinsociety.blogspot.com/2010/10/impact-on-modern-society.html

~Also from Bill Giovannetti~

Meet your Inner Brat, Inner Thug, Inner Loser, and Inner Jerk.
Do you ever feel as if aliens have landed inside your head and taken over? What about those words you blurted out and instantly regretted? Or those choices you repeated even though you swore you would never do them again? Meet the Dark Side of your soul... what the Bible calls your **Flesh**.

In the Inner Mess book, Bill Giovannetti reveals your supernatural divine resources to rise above the pull of the flesh. Scan the QR code for FREE SAMPLE CHAPTERS.

HOW TO KEEP YOUR INNER MESS FROM TRASHING YOUR OUTER WORLD

Creating peace from your inner chaos

Foreword by Dr Gary Benedict, President, Christian and Missionary Alliance

Bill Giovannetti

www.InnerMess.com

What Readers Say...

- "I'm still reading this book. It's one of the best Christian self help books out there!"

- "Discusses every day struggles in a realistic, to the point, sometimes humorous way... captivating!"

- "I've read many authors, but I can't put this one down!"

- "Bill, addresses all those distinctly "non-Christian" impulses we feel on a day-to-day basis and gives very practical advice on how to release the guilt, embrace Christ's incredible love for us, and live differently through the power of the Holy Spirit!"

powered by BWSCAN.com

An education should do more
than inform your mind... it
should ignite your heart too.
Train at Simpson University for a
lifetime of scholarship, relationship, and world service.
Fully accredited.
23 majors.
ROTC option.
Financial Aid Available.
Majestic. Surroundings.

CHALLENGE YOUR MIND
CHANGE YOUR WORLD
www.SimpsonU.edu

A.W. TOZER THEOLOGICAL SEMINARY

*"What comes into our minds when we think about God is the most important thing about us." --*A.W. TOZER

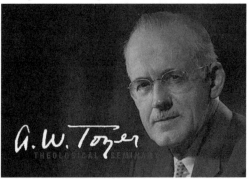

The focus at A. W. Tozer Theological Seminary is to teach students, to love students, to help students, and to pray for students as they become graduates who go into the world as disciple-making witnesses of Christ, giving to others from the treasures of Christ, all to the

tozer.simpsonu.edu   *glory of God.*

PAN AFRICAN ACADEMY OF CHRISTIAN SURGEONS

A portion from your purchase of this book supports PAACS, equipping a new generation of African surgeons committed to staying in Africa and serving God among the world's neediest people.